A Color Guide to MacOS Ventura for Seniors

A GUIDE TO MACBOOKS, IMACS, AND IMAC MINIS (WITH MACOS VENTURA, VERSION 13) WITH COLOR GRAPHICS

Scott La Counte

RIDICULOUSLY SIMPLE BOOKS

ANAHEIM, CALIFORNIA

www.RidiculouslySimpleBooks.com

Table of Contents

Disclaimer: Please note, while every effort has been made to ensure accuracy, this book is not endorsed by Apple, Inc. and should be considered unofficial.

INTRODUCTION

Are you new to macOS? Or maybe just upgrading to the newest OS? Whatever the case may be, this **full color** guide will help you learn the most powerful features of the latest macOS (Ventura).

It's going to cover new things like Stage Manager and Continuity Camera; but it will also walk you through the basics and help you discover things that you may not have known about.

Seeing images in B&W is helpful, but over the years, I've discovered that many readers prefer to see them in full color as they appear in real life; this manual was created from a B&W version that I am also selling.

Inside you will learn about:

- **What's new with iMac**
- **What's new to macOS Ventura**
- **How you do all those Windows "things" on a Mac**
- **Stage Manager**
- **Using Siri**
- **Setting up Internet and Email**
- **Using Sidecar**
- **Using Control Center**
- **Downloading / Updating apps**

- **Organizing photos**
- **Using Safari and Tab Groups**
- **Protecting your privacy**
- **Managing your passwords**
- **Sending, replying, and pinning messages**
- **Multitasking**
- **Using Live text**
- **And much, much more!**

Are you ready to start enjoying the new macOS? Then let's get started!

Chapter 1: What Exactly is "Mac"

Before diving into the actual software, let's address the obvious: why pick Mac?

I was in the Windows camp for a long time; I'd see the Mac and think it was just a computer for hipsters. Sure they were nice to look at—they were shiny and didn't look plastic-y and cheap…but they were also expensive.

But then I actually used one, and I was blown away. Here's why…

Fewer Viruses

You've probably heard someone say they use a Mac because they don't get viruses. That's not true. Any computer can get a virus. But it is true that Macs are generally less prone to viruses and are more secure.

The reason you don't hear about Mac viruses very often is twofold:

While it's hard to pinpoint just how many computers there are in the world, most computers are still Windows. So, if you are a hacker wanting to wreak havoc into cyberspace, then your obvious target would be the one with the largest audience.

The second reason is MacOS is built by Apple, for Apple. Windows builds their OS to be built for essentially any computer, which opens the door for vulnerabilities.

I know a lot of Mac users and rarely do I hear someone say they have a virus. If you are concerned, however, one popular free virus protector is called Bitdefender Virus Scanner (http://www.bitdefender.com/).

Keeping It Simple

When it comes to design, Apple likes to make things that are beautiful and simple. This philosophy can be seen in their watches, iPhones, and iPads—across all their products.

Because Apple spends so much time keeping it simple, you also have seen the last days of computer crashes and blue screens of deaths.

Apple spends a lot of time thinking not just about what the computer should do, but how people will do it. If you've been using Windows all of your life, then all the different menus and buttons might seem intimidating at first—but don't stress! This book will show you how much easier it actually is.

If you have any other Apple products, then many of the common Mac tasks will probably seem very similar to you. What's more, if you have an iPhone, iPad, or even Apple TV, then they all work and interact with each other.

No Bloat

I remember my last Windows computer. I couldn't wait to turn it on…and then I couldn't wait to turn it off! Your first hour should be spent just having fun exploring it, but my first hour was spent uninstalling programs!

One reason Windows computers are cheaper is that manufacturers team up with software companies and install all kinds of unnecessary programs—most of them are just free trials.

With Mac, you turn your computer on for the first time, create an ID if you don't already have one, put in your Wi-Fi, and log in to iTunes / iCloud. That's it. It should take less than ten minutes to get your computer up and running once you get it out of the box.

What's the Deal With M?

Apple announced it was going to start making its own chip called Silicon. In November 2020, the chip was unveiled and it had an official name: M1.

Awesome, right! Jump up and down! Party like it's 1999! Or, if you're like most of the world shrug your shoulders and say: "What's the big deal!"

It's a fast chip, but who cares!

On the surface, the computer really looks no different than Macs without M1. But it's on the inside that counts: the hardware.

Yes, it is fast--like really fast! It opens things several times faster than any Mac out there. That means if you're opening a memory intensive software, you'll barely notice any delay from when you tap to open it and when it actually opens. You're a patient person and that doesn't matter? Well, it also improves battery life. You'll probably be able to make it through an entire day on a single charge.

So that's all great, but here's where things really get nice: it's made by Apple.

Prior to M1, Apple chips were made by other manufacturers. It's kind of like having someone else's heart inside you. Yeah, it works--and sure it keeps you alive. But there's nothing better than having your own heart. M1 means that nearly everything in that computer is made by Apple, for Apple. It makes it more efficient and with fewer room for error. In short: it means it's going to perform better.

One of the biggest advantages of having a chip made by Apple for Apple is it can run apps from other devices natively. That means you'll be able to go to the Mac App Store and install iOS apps right in MacOS.

In 2022, Apple released the M2 chip, which is several times faster. You'll probably start seeing the chip updated yearly.

Chapter 2: Switching Over From Windows

Let me preface this chapter by saying: it's not for everyone! Because many readers are Windows users switching to Mac, I think it's important to include a chapter to help you out. Not a Windows user? Just skip ahead.

So exactly how is Mac different from Windows? Throughout the book, I'll be making comparisons to help you, but first I want to give a rundown of some of the major differences.

If you have an old Windows USB mouse, you don't have to toss it—you can plug it into your Mac and it will work with no installation. The right-click will even work.

I'll explain how to customize your Trackpad later in the book, but if you'd like to jump ahead, you can go to System Preferences > Trackpad.

And don't worry about messing something up; it's very hard to harm a Mac!

Right Click

Right-clicking is probably second nature to you if you are a Windows user; on the Mac, it's all about gestures—touching the Trackpad (Mac's mouse) a certain way (or on new Macs, using more or less pressure) will bring up different options and menus.

As weird as it sounds, the first time I used a Mac, the right-click (or lack thereof) drove me crazy…until I figured out that right-clicking was actually there. To right-click on a Mac, click with two fingers instead of one. Alternatively, you can press Control and click with one finger.

Keyboard Shortcuts

This section will give you a very quick rundown of the more popular keyboard shortcuts; for a more detailed list, see Appendix A at the end of this book.

On a Windows computer, you might be used to using Control (CTRL) frequently; Control is on the Mac keyboard, but don't get confused—on a Mac, the Control button equivalent is the Command (⌘) Key (to the right of the keyboard). The good news is the letter combination for the most frequently used Windows shortcuts is almost always the same on a Mac—Control-C to copy is Command-C on the Mac; Control-X to Cut is Command-X; Control-V to Paste is Command-V.

On a Windows computer, you can hold Alt and Tab to cycle through programs...on a Mac you use Command and Tab.

The two most frequently used function keys (the buttons above the numbers) are F3 and F4; F3 will show a list of the programs you have open, and F4 brings up your Launchpad (all of your available programs...kind of like the Start menu on Windows).

Just keep reminding yourself that while it looks different, it's really not...Windows has File Explorer, Mac has Finder; Windows has the Start Menu, Mac has Launchpad; Windows has the Ribbon menu, Mac has the Top Navigation menu.

Below is a quick overview of what things are called on Windows and what they are called on a Mac:

Windows	Mac
Windows Explorer / My Computer / Computer	Finder
Control Panel	System Preferences
Programs	Applications (often shortened to apps)
Task Bar and Start Menu	Dock
Tray	Menulets
Recycle Bin	Trash
Task Manager	Activity Monitor
Media Center	iTunes

Transferring Documents

The thing a lot of people worry about when updating any computer is how to get all of your information from your old computer to your new computer. With Macs, it's a pretty simple task—you can even take it into your local Apple Store for free help (appointments are needed, so don't just walk in).

If you don't want to wait for an appointment or you just like doing things on your own, there's already a tool on your computer to help: it's called Migration Assistant. Be advised, you do need an Internet connection.

To start, go to your Windows computer and either search any search engine for "Windows Migration Assistant" or go directly to https://support.apple.com/kb/DL1557?locale=en_US. Once you are there, download and install the program on your Windows computer.

From your Mac, click the Launchpad icon (i.e. the rocket on your taskbar).

Next, click on Other and then click Migration Assistant.

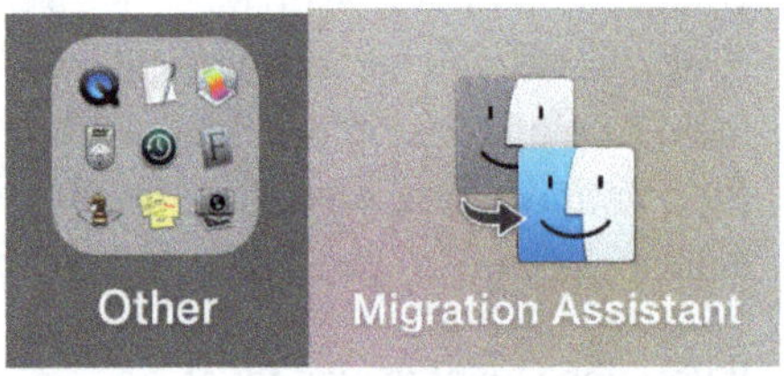

To use Migration Assistant, everything that is open on your Mac will be closed, so make sure and save your work, and don't start until you are ready.

From the setup, click Continue, and then select "From another Mac, PC, Time Machine backup, or other disk," then select Continue and then "From another Mac or PC." The next window should show the Windows computer that you want to transfer files from. Click Continue, verify on the Windows computer that the passcodes match and click Continue again. Lastly, the assistant will ask you to select the types of files you want to transfer.

If you don't do the assistant right away, you can always use it later. There's no timeline for using it, so if you dig up an older Windows computer in the garage and want to transfer everything from it, the option will always be there.

Compatibility

Now that you have everything copied over, let's talk briefly about compatibility. While many files will open on a Mac, the software will not. That means if you have Word on Windows, you can't just move it over; most popular software (like Word) is available on the Mac, but you will have to purchase it.

Don't stress too much; most the files that you have just transferred will actually still open even if you don't buy software to open them. Word files (Doc, Docx) for example, will open in Pages (which is free on new Macs).

If your file does not open, then you will probably be able to find free software online that will open it.

Setup Assistant

If you are starting up the Mac for the first time (and you are the first owner), then the first thing that will happen is an automated setup assistant will guide you through creating an account and getting everything set up.

The first thing you'll do is select your country; if you don't see yours, then click See All. Click Continue after you finish each section. Next, you'll choose your keyboard layout; if you are an English speaker, then the United States is probably your first bet, but if you are going to be typing primarily in another language (like Chinese) then you may want to pick that country instead—this can be changed later.

Picking the wireless network is the next thing you will see after clicking Continue—you don't have to set up wireless at this point, but if you do, it will also trigger the Migration Assistant (which will help you transfer files); this is all optional so you can skip it (you can also come back to it later).

The next screen is one of the most important: entering your Apple ID. If you have any other Apple devices (iPad, iPod, iPhone, etc.) or if you have an ID that you use with Windows, then you'll want to use it because all of the apps, music and other media you've paid for are tied to your account. If you don't have one, you'll have the option of getting one—it's free and includes iCloud (also free), which I'll be talking about later.

The next part of the setup is Find My Mac (which you need iCloud for); this is a great feature that lets you see where your Mac is from your Internet browser; if it's been stolen it also lets you wipe away all of your content.

After agreeing to the terms, you'll be taken to the Time Zone selection. After that, you are asked if you want to enable the iCloud Keychain. What's the iCloud Keychain? Basically, this stores passwords in the Cloud so you can use them on any device.

Next, decide if you want to send diagnostics and usage data to Apple; this is all for statistical purposes to help Apple make their software and hardware better, but it's entirely up to you. It won't slow your computer down if you do decide to do it—it's all done in the background. After this step, you decide if you want to register your installation with Apple.

Finally, you are ready to start using your Mac!

Chapter 3: What Exactly Is Ventura?

Ventura OS is the latest operating system available for Macs. While Ventura is free, it is not available to all devices; if you have an older Mac, then it may be time to upgrade to get all the best new features. The following devices are compatible, as of this writing:

- iMac - Late 2015 and later
- iMac Pro - 2017 and later
- MacBook Air - Early 2015 and later
- MacBook Pro - Early 2015 and later
- Mac Pro - Late 2013 and later
- Mac mini - Late 2014 and later
- MacBook - Early 2016 and later

It should also be noted that not all features are available on older models. So if you hear someone talking about a great new feature on their Mac and you don't see it, then it's probably because you have an older Mac.

If you aren't sure what model number you have, go the Apple icon in the upper left corner of your screen, then click About This Mac.

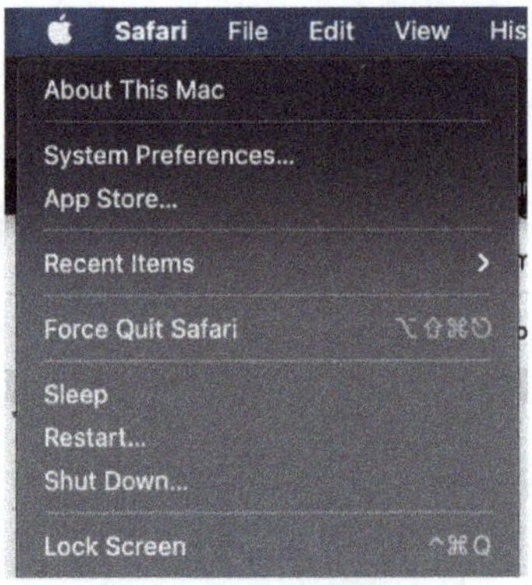

This will show you what OS you're running, the type of computer you have, and the serial number.

What's New?

If you are invested into Apple's ecosystem, then you'll love how familiar all their devices are—yes, they're different sizes and shapes, but the features on one are often nearly identical on others.

Messages has several new features including editing a message (but only for the first 15 minutes); unsending a message (but only for the first two minutes), marking a message as unread, and recovering deleted messages up to 30 days later. With SharePlay for messages, you can also synchronize movies, music and more with friends over iMessage. Unsend messages also comes to the iPad mail app: Mail--in addition to schedule send, follow-up, and remind me.

Spotlight (this how you search for things in macOS) has added the ability to search for more than just files--you can search for images, web results and much more.

If you liked Tab Groups on Monterey, you'll love it on Ventura; you can now share those tab groups with friends; so if, for example, you are planning a vacation with others, you can share a tab group so you are all on the same page.

One of the big highlights of iPadOS is Stage Manager. Stage Manager lets you resize apps into windows and makes it easier to multitask.

These are just some of the bigger upgrades, but there's smaller tweaks that will be covered In this book.

Chapter 4: It's Time to Learn the Basics of MacOS

The best way to learn is by doing, so I'm sure you're eager to get your hands wet and start using the Mac! If you are new to Mac, however, that can be a little intimating—it's not hard to use, but you have to, at the very least, know what you are looking at. In this chapter, I'll give you a crash course in the MacOS interface. By the end of the chapter, you won't be an expert, but you'll know where things are and how to start opening and using things.

Keyboard

The keyboard?! I know what you're thinking: a keyboard is a keyboard! Well, sort of. While it is true that you could use a Windows keyboard on a Mac, there are keyboards (including the one that's free with your Mac or built into your MacBook) that are specifically designed for Mac.

There are not a lot of differences; below are the four main ones.

Apple Key

On a Windows keyboard, there is a button that looks like a Windows flag called the Windows Button. There's no sense putting a Windows button on a Mac keyboard, so where the Windows button normally is, you'll find the Apple button, which doesn't look at all like an apple! It actually looks like this (⌘); it's more commonly known as the Command Button—though some people also call it the Clover Key and Pretzel Key.

Delete (Backspace)

On a Windows keyboard, the backspace button is a 'Backwards Delete' key and the delete button is a 'Forward Delete' key (removing the space immediately after the cursor). On a Mac keyboard, the backspace key is labeled 'Delete' and is in exactly the same location as the Windows backspace key. Most Mac keyboards don't have a Forward Delete key anymore, though larger ones do—it's called "Del->". If you don't see it, you still can use forward delete by hitting the FN button (button left corner of your keyboard) and Delete button.

The Desktop

Hopefully, by now, your files are transferred, you've completed the initial startup, and you have a pretty picture on your desktop. At last, you are ready to use your computer!

The desktop is where you'll be spending much of your time, so let's take some time getting to know it.

The first thing you should notice is that it's really not that much different from Windows—it's a vast space that you can either leave empty or fill with icons or documents.

Dark Mode

Deep in the halls of Apple, developers have been working on something very...dark. It's called Dark Mode. Does anyone want to guess what happens when you switch it on? If you said "Disney emoji's dance happily on your screen" then go back and reread the question. So, what is dark mode and why would you want to use it?

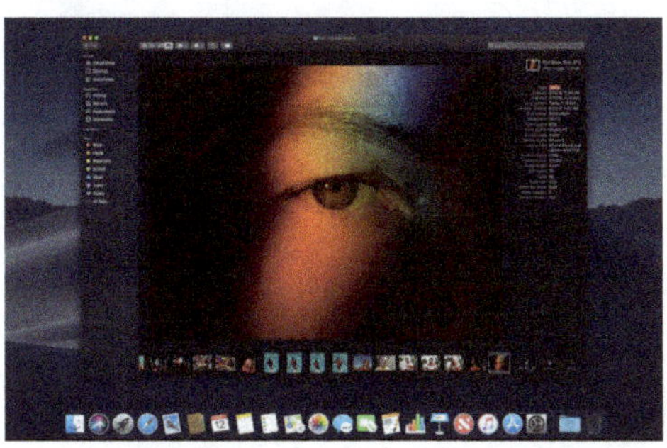

The point of dark mode is to put an emphasis on what you are working on or what you need to find. Let's say you're editing a photo. What's important? The photo. All those things in the background are just noise. Sometimes you need the noise for what you're working on, but you'll work more effectively by having them darkened. It's not like things in the background are harder to see—the contrast just helps you be more creative. At least that's what Apple thinks. If you think otherwise, you have the option to turn it off.

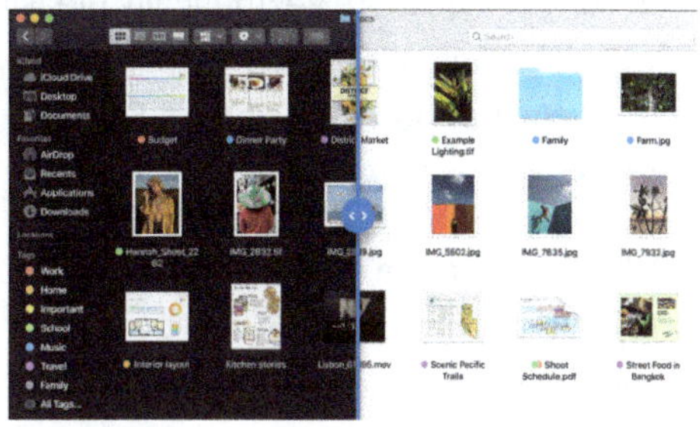

In the image above, you can see the difference between dark mode (left) and light mode (right). In dark mode, those thumbnails should pop a little more than in light mode.

Not all apps will look different. It's up to the company that makes the app to redesign an app that takes advantage of it. Apple has obviously updated many of its apps (like Calendar, iTunes, Mail).

If you've updated to MacOS Catalina then you'll be asked if you want it on. If you want to turn it on, or if you turned it off but now want it on, it's easy to do:

Go to System Preferences (you'll find that in the app launch area of your Dock).

Select General and select the option.

When you're in System Preferences > General, you'll also notice you have the option to change the accent color that goes along with light / dark mode; this changes all the arrows, toggles, etc. throughout the OS. You can always go back to default settings, so don't be afraid to play around: you won't break anything!

It's Dynamic!

Apple always likes to put emphasis on making things more aesthetically pleasing when they update the OS. Dark mode is one way they do that; Dynamic Desktop is another.

When I heard the name, I imagined it would let your wallpaper come alive by having something more...dynamic—like the wallpaper could be a looped video or something. It's a little less dynamic than that, unfortunately, but still a cool feature.

So what is it? Well, the wallpaper on your desktop will change, but it's a little slower. Basically, the wallpaper changes appearance depending on what time of day it is. So in Apple's example, there's an image of the Mojave desert; in the morning it's bright and throughout the day it gets darker.

To use it, make sure you have Location Series on—the OS has to know what time it is in your time zone.

Stacked

Mac excels in many ways; one of the biggest ways is in how it keeps you organized. Apple is always working hard thinking about how to help you stay organized and keep all your content structured in a way that makes it easy to find.

Apple is a bit like a library; other OSes are a bit like used bookstores. Both places have the same thing: books. But one is organized in a way to help you find what you need quickly; the other is organized in a way where you really need to browse for things.

If your desktop looks a little like the below image, then Stacks can help.

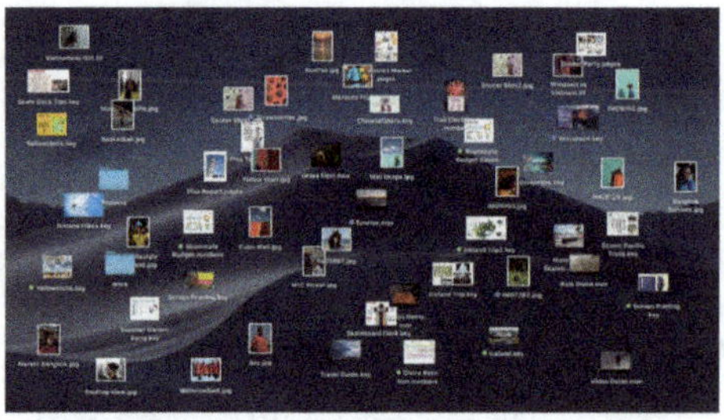

How does Stacks clean this mess up? When it's enabled, the above screenshot would look a bit like the below one.

Everything is still there, but it's grouped together. All the images, documents, and movies are in one group. If you want to see anything within that group, then just click the thumbnail and it will expand. If you add a new file to your desktop, it's automatically put in the appropriate group.

If you're on your desktop, you can turn it on by clicking and selecting Use Stacks. You can also do this by going into Finder and then choosing Use Stacks. You can also pick how you want things stacked. By default, it's by kind, but you can also stack by date or tag.

If you want to turn it off, repeat the process above but uncheck Use Stacks.

Menu Bar

One of the most noticeable differences between Windows and Mac on the desktop is the top menu bar. I'll be referring back to this menu bar throughout the book, but right now what you need to know is this bar changes with each program that you open, but some of the features remain the same. The little apple, for instances, never changes—clicking on this will always bring up options to restart, shut down, or log out of your computer. The little magnifying glass at the far right is also always there. Any time you click on that, you can search for files, emails, contacts, etc., that are on your computer.

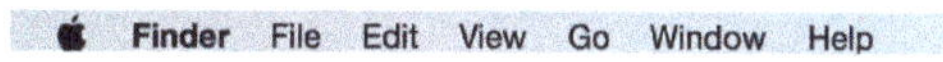

Spotlight

Spotlight used to be the way you found files. It still is. But it's evolved too more than that. Type in a word or phrase (I use dog photos in the example below) and it begins searching for not only files, but web matches, documents where the phase is used within it, Siri suggestions, and more.

You can find Spotlight in the top right corner of your Mac—it's the little magnifying glass.

Menulets

At the top right, you'll see several "menulets," which include Bluetooth, wireless connectivity, volume, battery, time and date, the name of the account currently logged in, Spotlight, and Notifications, as well as other assorted third-party icons (if installed).

As this book continues, we'll refer back to this part of the menu.

Control Center

If you have other Apple devices, then you might notice that things on the Mac look a little familiar. That's on purpose. Each update, Macs add new features that resemble what you find on iPhones and iPads. It helps make the experience more friction-free, which makes it easier to get things up and running.

This is especially true with the Control Center, which is on the top menu right next to the Siri icon. Clicking on it will bring up a series of options. This is where you can change the Wi-Fi, mirror your screen, and more.

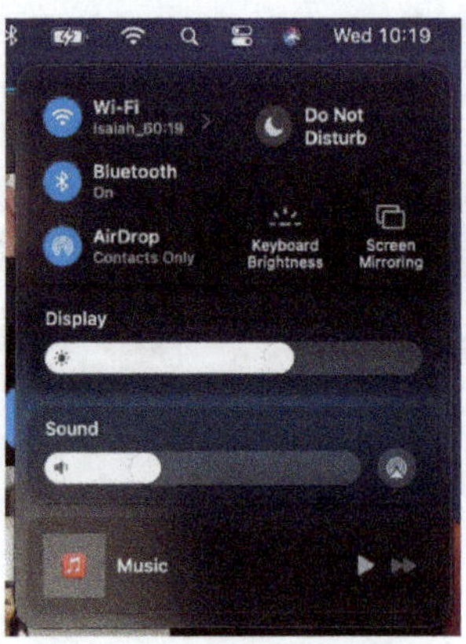

It may not look like a lot of options, but each control has subcontrols. Just click on the arrow next to it.

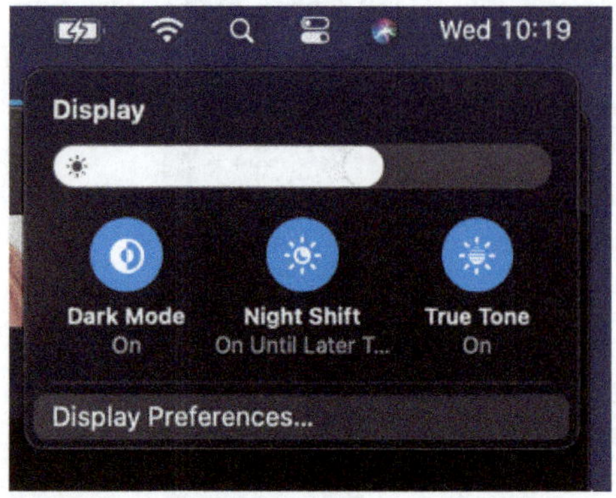

Dock

Windows has a taskbar on the bottom of the screen, and Mac has a Dock; the Dock is where all your commonly used applications are.

If you see a little dot under the icon, then the program is currently open. If you want to close it, then click the icon with two fingers to bring up the options, and then click Quit.

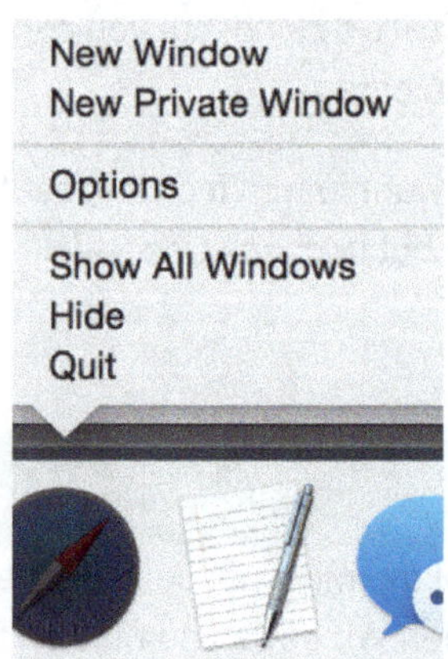

Removing a program from the Dock is pretty simple—just drag the icon to the Trash and let go. This will not remove the program—it only removes the shortcut. Finder, Trash, and Launchpad are the only programs that you cannot remove.

If you want to add a program to the Dock, then open it; when the icon appears on the Dock, click with two fingers, then go to Options and select Keep in Dock.

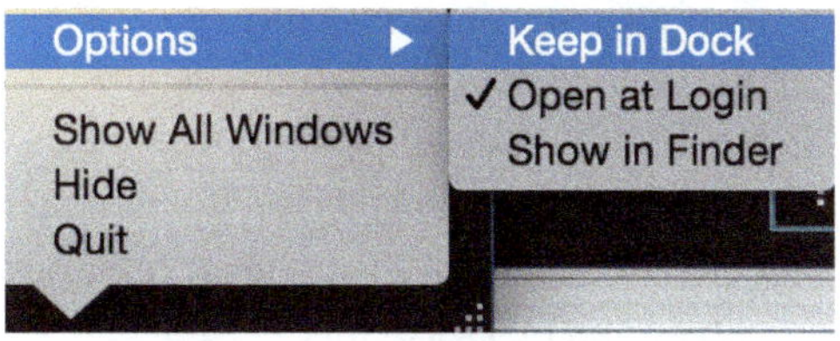

Trash

At the right end of the Dock is the Trash. To delete a folder, file or application, drag the item to the Trash, or right-click (two-finger click) the item and select Move to Trash from the pop-up menu. If you want to eject a disk or drive, such as an iPod or USB flash drive, drag the volume into the Trash. As the volume hovers over the Trash, the icon morphs from a trash can to a large eject button. Release the mouse, and your volume will be safely ejected and can be removed from the computer. To empty the Trash, right-click (click with two fingers) on the Trash icon in the Dock, and select Empty Trash.

You can manage the Trash yourself, but I also highly recommend an app called "Clean My Mac" (https://macpaw.com/cleanmymac); it's a little expensive, but when I use it, it normally helps me free up 1GB of storage just by deleting installation files and extensions that I don't need.

App Buttons

The little lights in the image above have no name. Some people call them traffic lights. You'll start seeing a lot of them because nearly all Mac programs use them. On a Windows, you've seen them as an X and a minus in the upper right of your screen. On a Mac, they appear in the upper left of the running program. The red light means close, the yellow light means minimize, and the green makes the app full screen.

Full screen means the program takes up the entire screen and even the Dock disappears. You can see the Dock and other programs quickly by swiping the Trackpad to the right with four fingers. To get back to the app, swipe with four fingers to your left.

Launchpad

Launchpad is essentially the Start menu on a Windows computer. It shows your programs.

When you click it, you'll see rows of programs; you can immediately start typing to search for an app, or you can just look for it. If you have a lot of apps, then you probably have more than one screen. Swipe with two fingers to the left to see the next screen.

Launchpad takes a lot of cues from iPhone and iPad. If you want to remove a program, for example, you do it the same way you remove an iPhone or iPad app. Just click and hold until an X appears above it, then click the X to remove it. Similarly, to rearrange icons, use the same method for rearranging iPhone / iPad apps—click and hold over the icon until it begins to shake, and then move it wherever you want it to go. You can even put programs into groups the same way as an iPhone / iPad—click and hold over the icon, then drag it on top of the app you want to group it with; finally, when the folder appears, you can let go.

After you delete a program, you can re-download it anytime, by going into the App Store (as long as you downloaded it from the App Store and not from a website).

Notifications

For the past few updates, Apple has attempted to replicate iOS (iPad / iPhone) features; the move is meant to make using a Mac much like using a mobile device. This attempt at replicating features is especially true with Catalina OS.

Notification was a new feature to OS X Yosemite. You can find it on the top menu button at all times; it's to the far right-hand corner and looks like this:

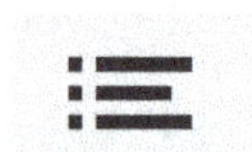

Click it any time you want to see alerts. You can also access it by swiping with two fingers to the left from the edge of your Trackpad.

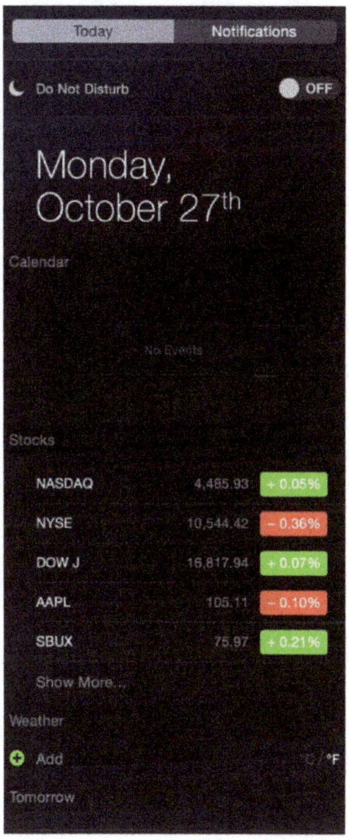

When you swipe down from the top of an iPad or iPhone you will get a similar screen. There are two parts of the Notifications menu: Today and Notifications.

The Today tab is where you'll see things happening more in the moment—what's the weather, what's in your calendar, what's going on with your stocks, etc. The Notifications tab is where you'll see things like Facebook messages or emails. Later in this book, I'll show you how to customize it.

Split View

Split view is perhaps the biggest added feature to OS X. It lets you run two apps side-by-side—but there's a catch: not all apps are compatible. So if you're scratching your head because this feature won't work for you, then chances are it's not that you are doing it wrong—it's that the app doesn't support the feature.

There are two ways to get the split view to work. Let's look at both of them. First, make sure the two apps that you want to run side-by-side are not running in full screen mode.

Method 1

Click and hold the green button in the upper left corner of your app.

A transparent blue box will appear; drag and drop the app into it (by default, the blue is on the left side, but if you drag to the right side, it will also turn blue and you can drop it in).

Next, click the program you want to use side-by-side.

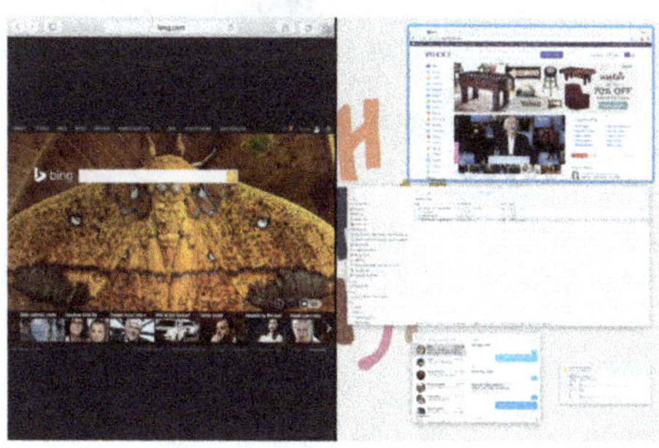

A side-by-side window now appears; you can use the middle black line to make one bigger or smaller, by dragging left or right.

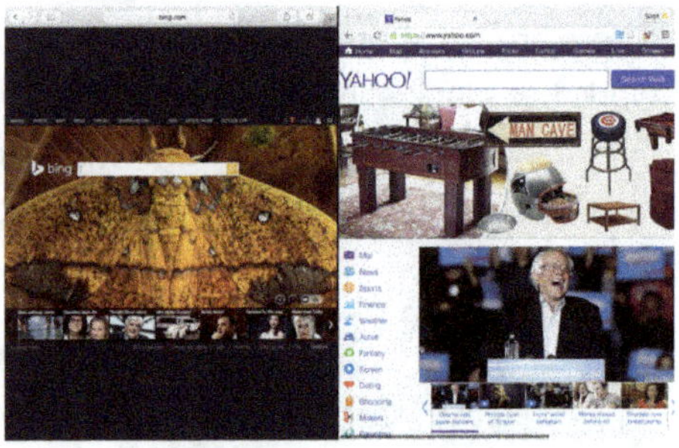

To return to the normal view, click the green button in the upper left corner of the app once more (you can also hit the ESC key on your keyboard).

Method 2

As you are probably noticing, most things in OS X can happen by several different methods; side-by-side view has two. The second way to get apps is to open your Mission Control, and drag the app to the top menu.

You'll notice, a grey box appears and the box appears to split.

Once you drop the app into that box, you'll see a side-by-side preview. Once you click the preview, it will maximize.

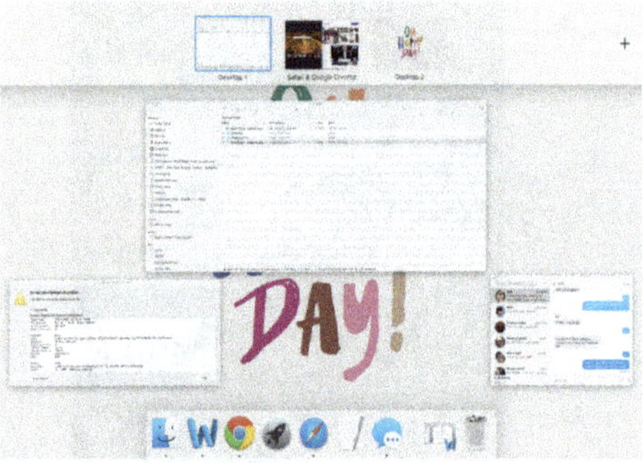

Returning to the non-split screen is done the same way as Method 1 (click the green box in the upper left corner or hit the ESC key on the keyboard).

Stage Manager

Stage manager is a way to multitask between apps. Look at the example below. Notice how there's several windows open in the background? Makes it hard to navigate around doesn't it?

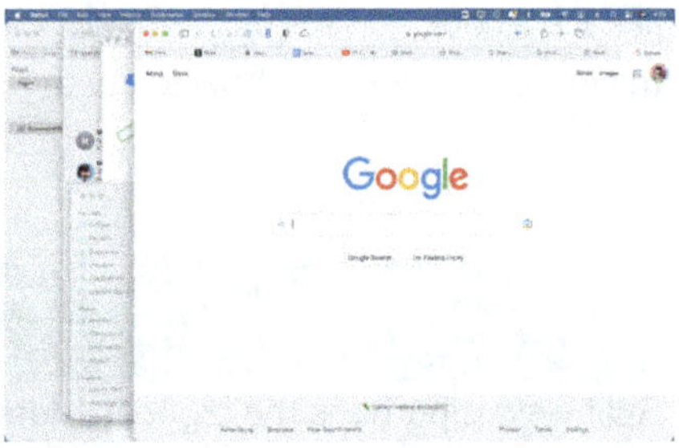

With Stage Manager turned on, it looks like the image below.

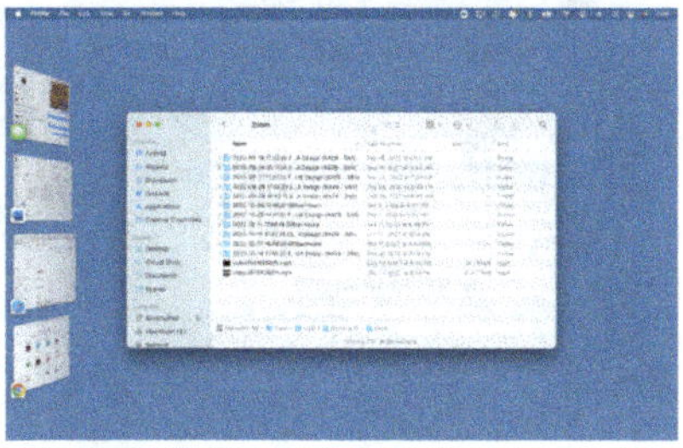

The thumbnails let you quickly toggle between the apps that you have open.

Go to the control center in the upper right corner of your screen to turn it on.

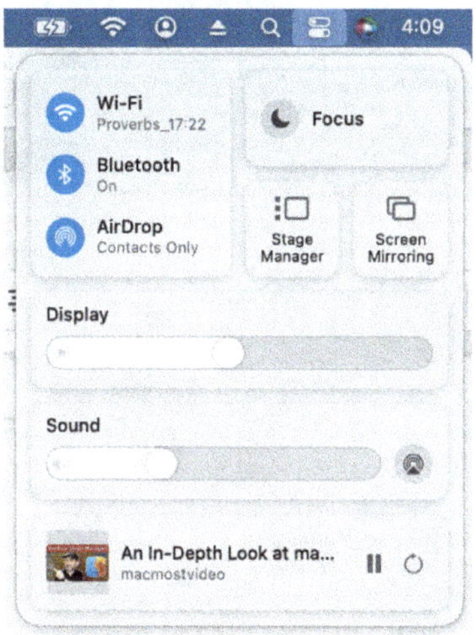

Press it again to turn it off. When you press it again, it will also give you the option for how you'd like to sort apps.

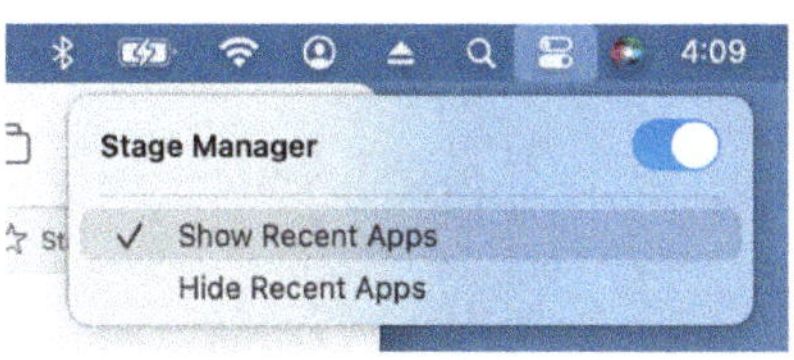

Tabbed Software

If you've ever used Tabs on Internet Explorer or Chrome, then this next feature might interest you. It allows you to open documents (such as Maps and Pages) with tab viewing. Note: not all Mac apps support this feature.

To use it, open two windows of the same app. I'll use Maps in the example below.

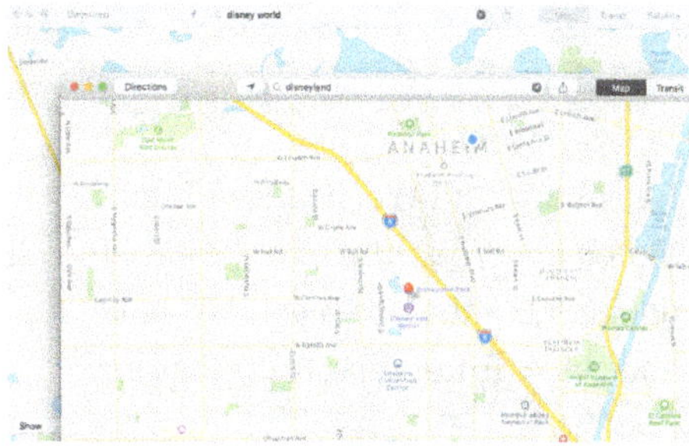

Next, go to Window and Merge All Windows.

Your windows should now be merged.

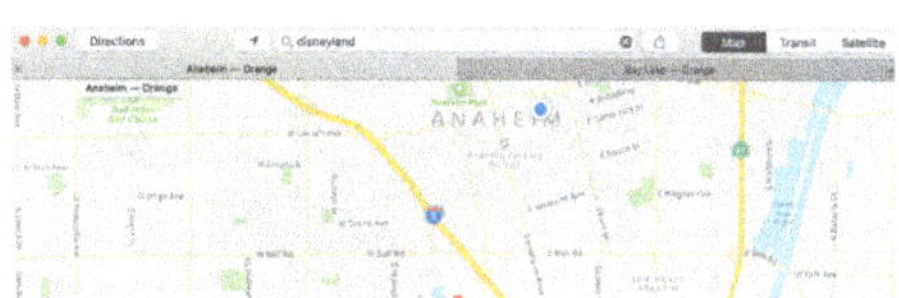

Picture-In-Picture Video

If you'd like to watch a video while you work, then you're in luck! If you already own the video (a video you purchased on iTunes, for example), then just start playing the video and go to View and Float on Top.

But what about Web videos? Such as Vimeo and YouTube? That's easy too. Just double-click the video you are watching, and select Enter Picture-In-Picture.

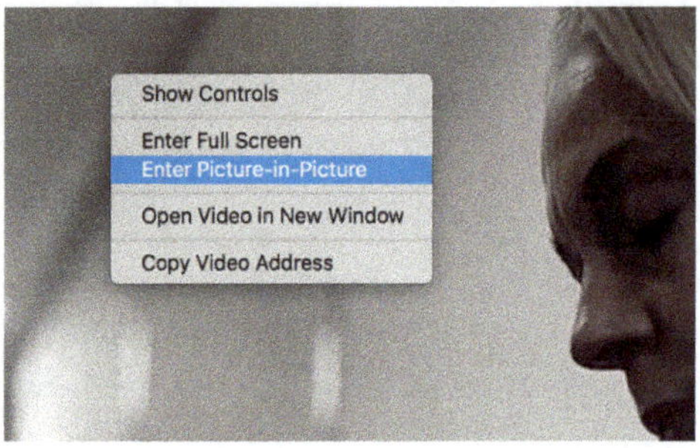

Your video will immediately begin playing above other windows.

Chapter 5: Where to Find Things

One of the greatest things about Mac is how easy it is to find things. Sure, Windows has a search, but it feels clunky and doesn't always work the way you expect. I'll cover how to find things in this chapter.

Finder

The first icon on your Dock—one of three that cannot be deleted or moved—is the Finder icon.

Finder is the Mac equivalent of Explorer on a Windows computer; as the name implies, it finds things. Finder is pretty resourceful and powerful so this section will be a little longer than others because there's a lot you can do with it.

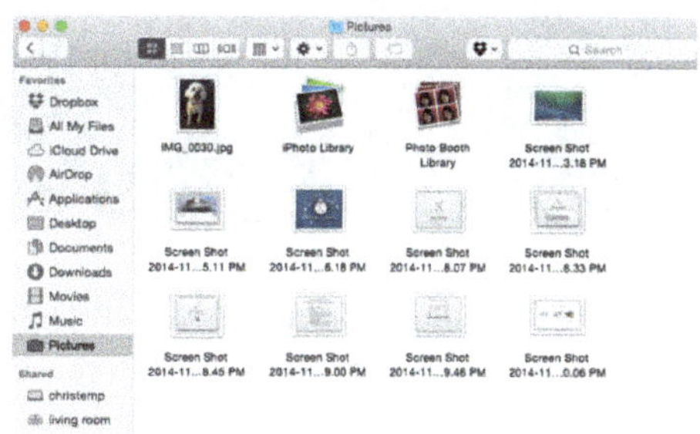

Let's get started by clicking on the Finder icon.

Finder Reimagined

Finder is how you find things on a Mac—clever name, right? Like a lot of things in MacOS, there are similarities between how it works on Mac and iPhone. Mojave added a few new features still present in Catalina you should know about, however.

Gallery View

There are several different types of views in Finder (where you find things—like File Explorer in Windows). Examples of views are: list, columns, and icons. Gallery view was a new view in Mojave that you still see in Catalina.

Gallery view displays a large preview of the file with thumbnails of everything else in the directory below it. And by "preview" this isn't just for images where you can see what the image looks like—this works across all kinds of docs. If it's a PDF, for example, you can see a preview of the PDF.

To the right of the file, there's a side panel that will tell you the more detailed metadata for the file.

Quick Actions

Apple is all about efficiency; to be more efficient, it helps to be able to do things a little quicker. That's where Quick Actions help. With Quick Actions, you can, for example, change the orientation of a file or add password protection. The actions available depend on the type of file.

Other Views

There are four other ways to view folders on your Mac—icons, lists, columns, and Cover Flow. Different views make sense for different file types, and you can change the view using the View Options icons (pictured below).

Cover Flow View

Cover Flow lets you quickly go through thumbnails / previews of photos (it's a little like Film Strip in Windows); you can also sort any of the columns by clicking on the header—so if you are looking for a larger file, then click the Size column, or if you are looking for a recent file, then pick the Date Modified column.

Icon View

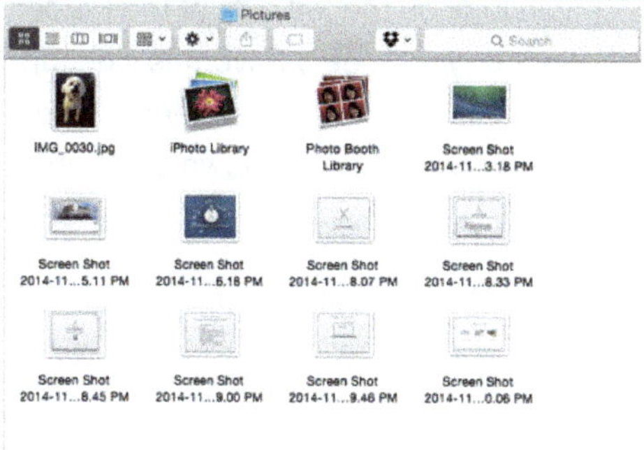

Icon View can help if you need to sort through several image files or applications. It gives you either a thumbnail of each picture or an icon for each file or app.

List View

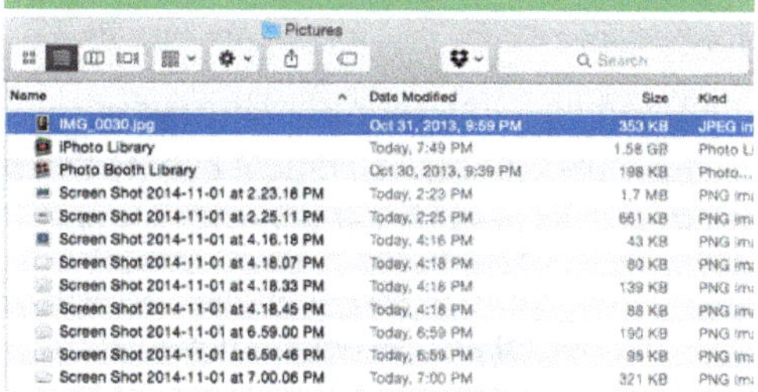

List View, on the other hand, gives you more information about the file, including the date it was last modified. This is the perfect view for sorting.

Column View

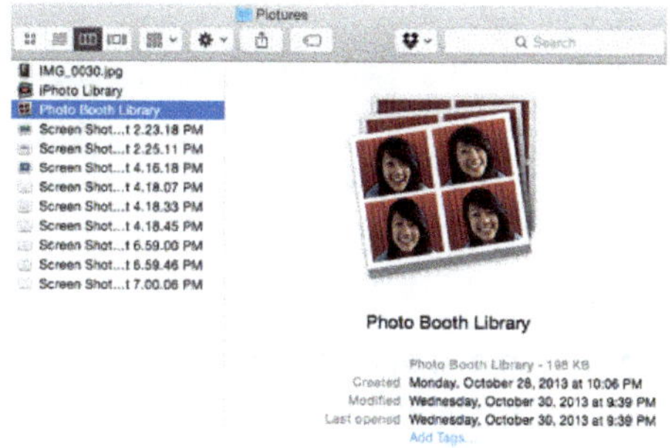

Finally, Column View which is kind of a hybrid of List View and Cover Flow View. It shows the folder hierarchy a file is located in. Notice that Finder doesn't include the Windows "go up one level" button—Column View is a good way to get the same results and navigate easily through your file structure.

Sorting in Finder

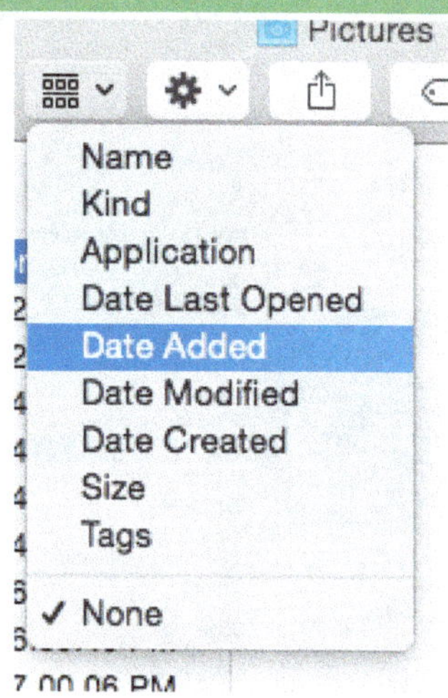

Finder gives you a number of ways to sort your files and folders. You can sort by name, type, the application required for opening the file (like Microsoft Word, for example), the date the file was created, modified, or opened, the file size, and any tags you may have applied.

File Management

Most file management tasks in OS X are similar to Windows. Files can be dragged and dropped, copied, cut and pasted. If you need to create a new folder, use the Gear icon in Finder, which will give you the option you need.

Catalina also allows you to batch rename files (i.e. rename several files at once instead of one at a time), potentially saving you hours of time, depending on your file system. To take advantage of this, select the files you'd like to rename (hint: use Command-click to select multiple files, or use Command-A to select everything). Then right-click (two-finger click) the selected files and choose "Rename X Items."

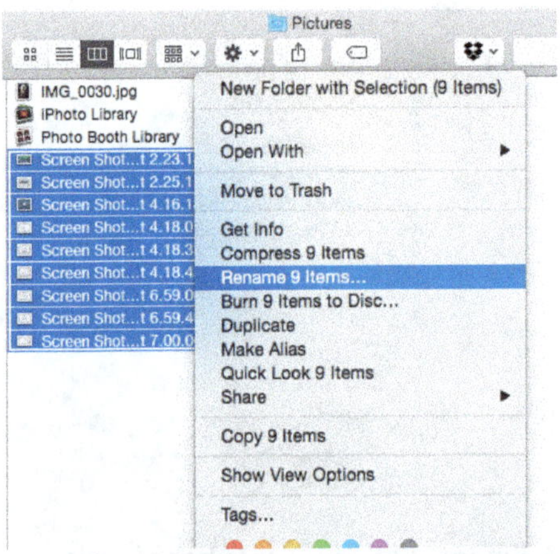

You'll then have the option to replace text or to add text to the file names.

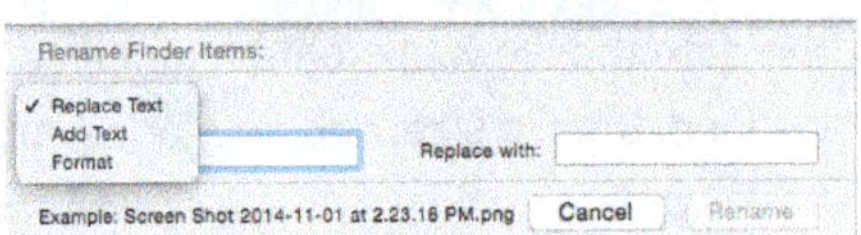

Favorites

If you look on the left side of the Finder Window, you'll see a Favorites sidebar. This section includes high-frequency folders, like Documents, Pictures, Downloads, and more.

To add an application or file to your Favorites menu, just drag it over to the Favorites area and drop it. To remove an item from Favorites, right-click it (click with two fingers) and select Remove From Sidebar.

Tabbed Browsing

Apple took a page from Internet browsers by adding something called "Tabbed Browsing" to Finder. Basically, instead of having several Finder boxes open (which is how you had to do it in older OSes) you open tabs. To open an additional Finder tab, press Command-T or click File and New Tab.

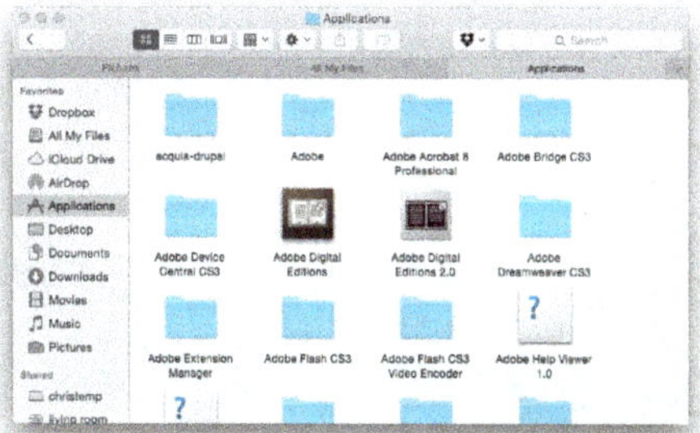

If you want to merge all of your tabbed windows, just click Windows in the file menu on the top of your screen, and then Merge All Windows.

TAGS

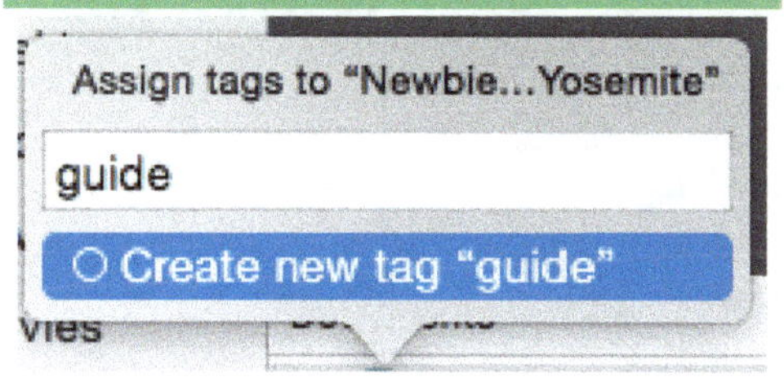

If you use photo apps like Flickr, then you probably know all about tagging; it's essentially adding subjects to your file to make it easier to find. Let's say the file is regarding the 2015 tax year—you can add a tag to the file called "2015 Taxes" or whatever you want it to be. You can also color code it.

To assign a tag to a file (you can also assign it to a folder), click the file / folder with two fingers, and then click tags; if this is your first tag just type it in and hit Enter; if you've already tagged a file and want to use the same name, then click the name of the tag as it appears.

Chapter 6: Let's Learn How to Get Things Done In MacOS

The Mac is a beautiful machine, but you can only admire that desktop for so long; eventually, you'll want to get on the Internet—how else will you get your daily dose of cat memes or keep in touch with the Nigerian prince trying to give you money? I'll show you how in this chapter.

There are two methods: Ethernet (i.e. plugging in a LAN cable to your computer) and Wireless.

Setting Up With Ethernet

All new Mac computers are set up with Wi-Fi; iMacs also have Ethernet ports to plug in a network cable. This option isn't available on any of the Mac laptops—though you can buy an adapter if you absolutely must have it.

If you have a basic Internet modem, then set up is pretty easy. Just plug a network cable into your Internet hub, and plug the other end into your Mac. Once it's plugged in, the Internet should work.

Newer Macs come with top of the line wireless radios for Wi-Fi, so you should be perfectly fine without using the Ethernet port.

Setting Up Wireless Networks

Setting up a wireless connection is also pretty simple. Just click the Wi-Fi menu on the menu bar. It looks like the image below and is near the upper right corner:

As long as there's a wireless network in range, it will show up when you click it (sometimes it does take a few seconds to appear).

If there's a lock next to the Wi-Fi name, then you'll need to know the passcode (if it's a home Internet connection, then it's usually on the bottom of your Internet modem; if it's at a business, then you'll have to ask for the code. If there's no lock, then it's an open network. You usually see this kind of network at places like Starbucks.

If it's a locked network, then as soon as you click on it, it will ask for the code; once it's entered and you click Connect, then you're connected (assuming you added it right); if it's not locked then once you click on it, it will attempt to connect.

Safari

If you've used Safari before, it's probably going to look a little different for you. In 2021, Apple gave Safari a facelift to make it even more resourceful. It's great on the MacOS, but even better when you have an entire ecosystem of devices (i.e. iPad and iPhone).

Let's dig into the anatomy of the browser, then I'll break down how it works.

The top toolbar looks pretty bare. Looks can be deceiving because there's a lot here. Starting on the far left is the side menu button, which brings up your Saved Tabs (more on that later), private viewing mode, history and more; the middle is where you can either type or search for the website (the microphone lets you say it instead of type it), and finally the Plus button lets you open a new tab.

Tabs don't look like tabs in MacOS. In the example below, there are three opened tabs. The middle one is the opened website, the smaller two (Start Page and Amazon) are the opened, non-active, tabs.

There are a few ways to close a tab. One is to tap the X next to the website name (this is only on the active tab); the other way is right-clicking on the tab, then selecting to close the tab.

When you click and hold over the Plus button, you'll see a list of recently closed tabs that you can open again.

If you need to open a private tab (meaning a tab window that doesn't keep track of your passwords or history—it's great for gift shopping if you share a device), then go to File>New Private Window.

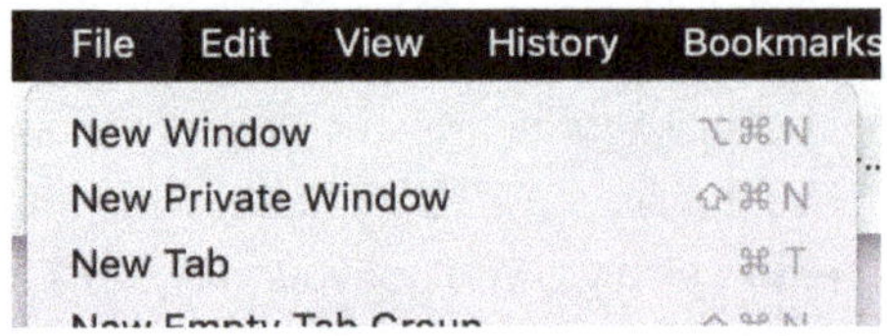

Website Options

When you click the three dots on the page you are currently visiting, you'll get several more options. This is where you'll go if you want to add the page to your Bookmark or add it to your Favorites (Favorites show up whenever you start Safari when it's been closed—it's known as your "Start Page." You can also share the page with someone, change the text size, and see a Privacy Report. Privacy Report shows all the trackers on a page, so you know what information a company is collecting about you.

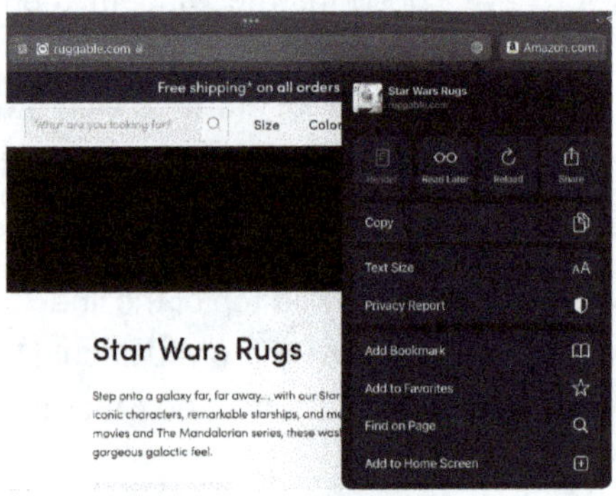

Menu Options

On the far left side is the option to bring up the menu pane. The menu can be shown as you browse, or you can collapse it once you pull up what you are looking for.

There are a few things you can do here. First is Group Tabs; there's a lot to Group Tabs, so I'll go over it in the next section.

Start Page is your homepage; Private turns your browser into a private web surfing experiences where your web history and passwords aren't saved.

Shared With You

Shared With You is where you'll see things that have been shared recently. As an example: my wife and I share a lot of links through text. When she sends one, they'll automatically show up here. That way, I don't have to search through dozens of texts to find the page she mentioned—it's already been saved.

If you want to remove the link, then tap and hold your finger on the page preview. This brings up several options—one is remove. You can also use the options here to reply to the message, open in the background or copy the link.

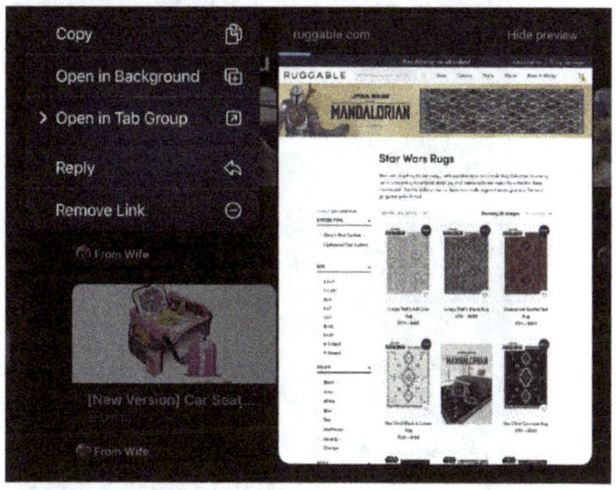

Safari Bookmarks

Below Shared With You are the Bookmarks; Bookmarks are pages you save because you regularly go to them. When you start getting a lot of Bookmarks, it's a good idea to put them into organized folders.

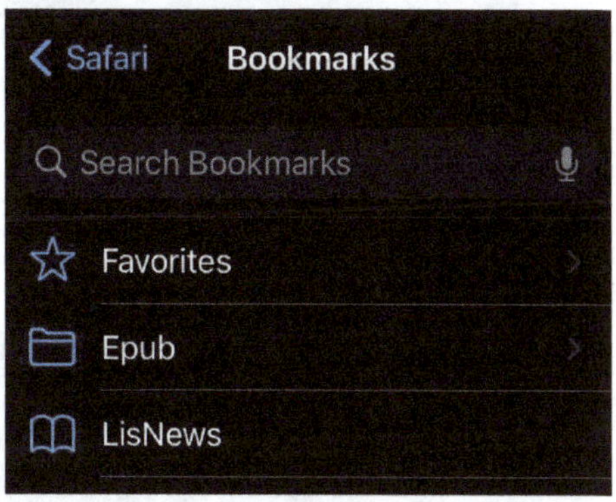

To create a folder, just go to the bottom of the page to Edit, then select New Folder. When you have selected Edit, you can also delete Bookmarks and move them into folders.

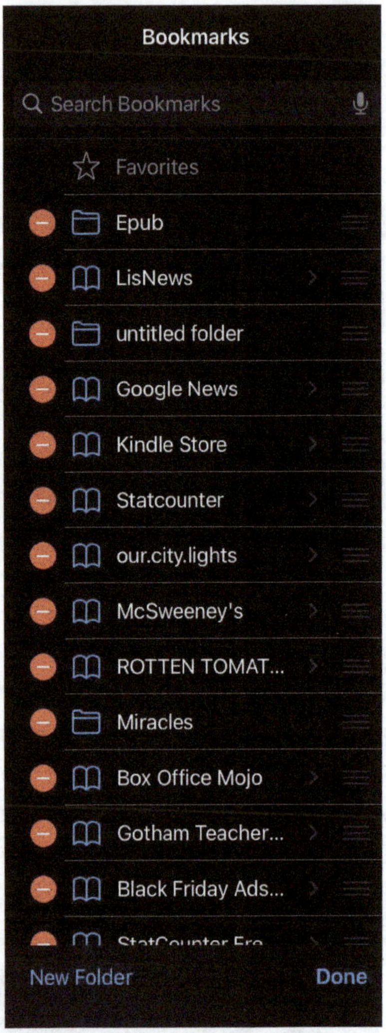

You can put folders into folders when you create them.

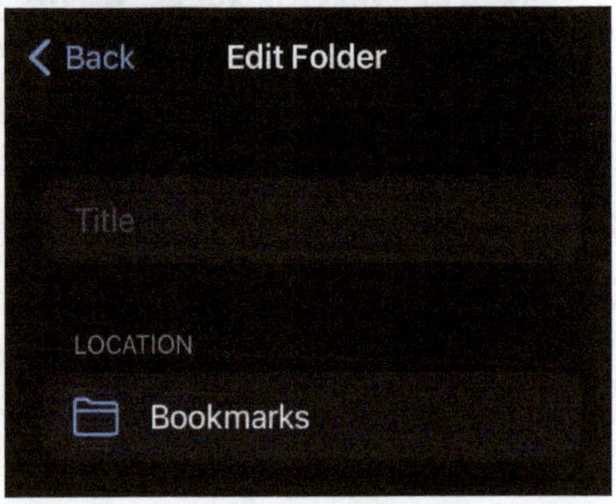

Web History

If you are not using Private mode, then all your history is saved; this is helpful if you ever forget a website you went to, but you know what day you went to it. If you ever want to clear your history, just tap the Clear option at the bottom of the page when you are viewing your history.

Tab Group

Tabs can be your best friend. Tab Group is the evolution of this friend. Tab Groups are kind of a combination of bookmarks and tabs. You basically save all your tabs into a group. So, for example, you can have a group called "Shopping" and when you click it, like magic, all your favorite shopping websites open into tabs.

To get started, open all the tabs that you want to be in your group, then go to the left menu, and click on the + button from the side menu and select New Empty Tab Group.

Type in the name of your group. Remember to be descriptive, so you know what your Tab Group is for.

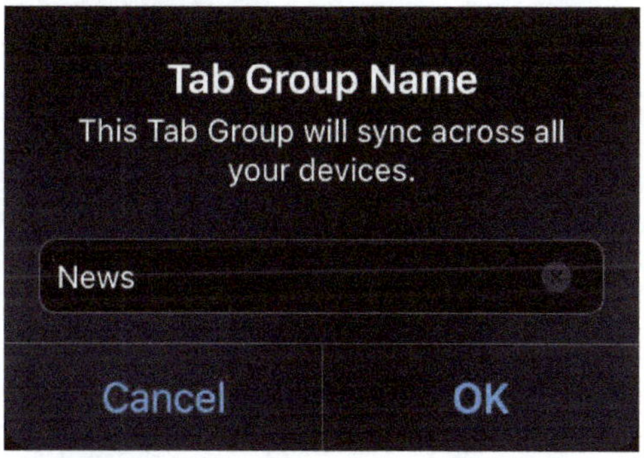

All the tabs are now saved in your group; in the example below, there are two tab groups; when I toggle between them, new tabs will open.

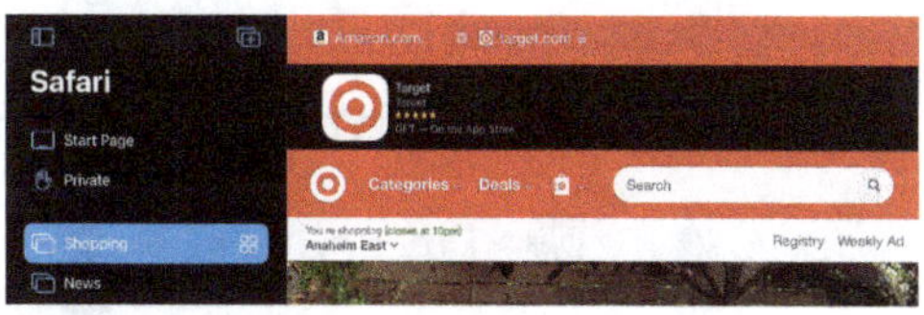

You can make changes to your group by tapping and holding on it.

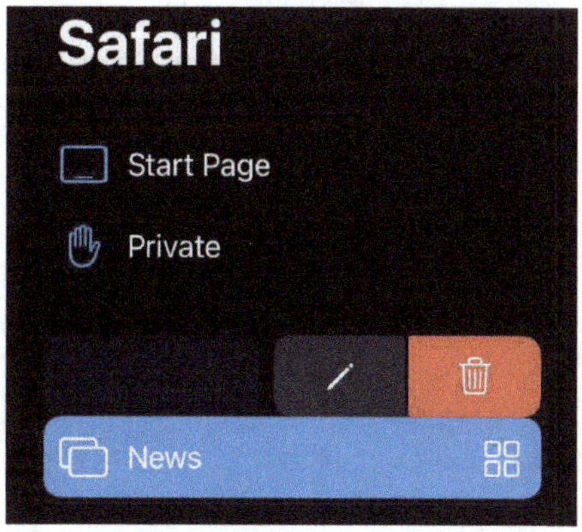

If you want a new tab to show there, just open up the tab while in that group and it will automatically be saved in the group.

Focus

Computers can distract us from things we need to be doing. To help you, there is a Focus mode. To access it, click the control panel in the upper right corner of the screen, then click Focus.

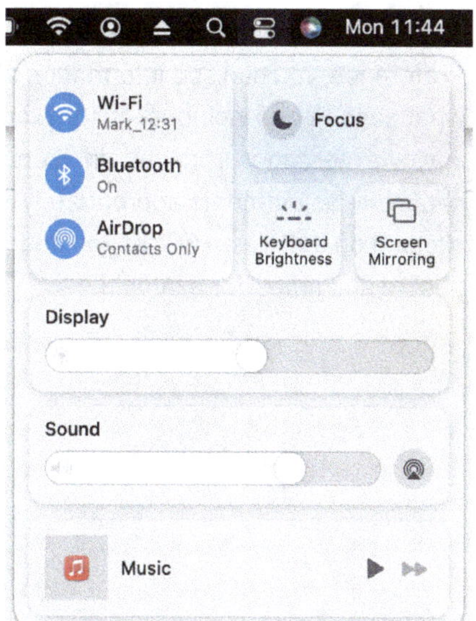

There are several different Focus modes—each with different settings. Some will send you notifications, but not calls, for example.

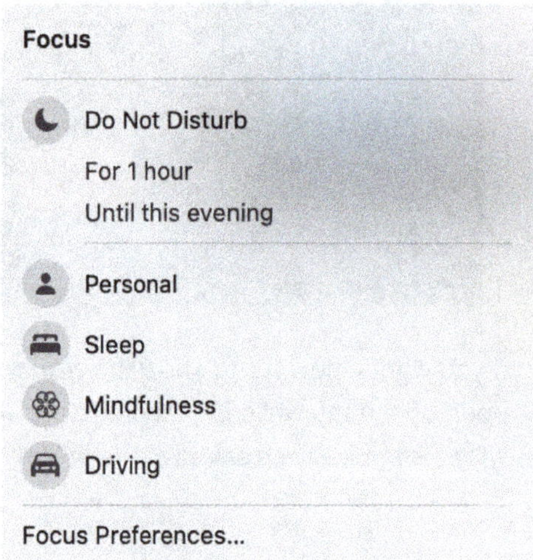

When you click on your Focus, you can select how long you want it on for.

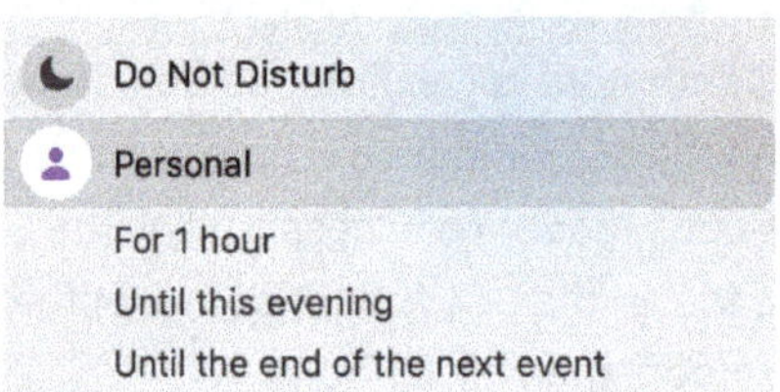

If you click the last option, Focus Preference, you can see information about what each Focus includes—if, for example, it allows messages from certain users. You can make adjustments appropriately—clicking on the + icon will let you add people and times, for example.

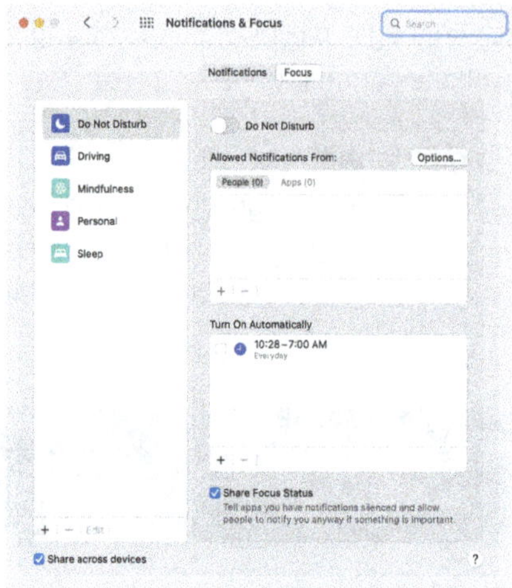

You can add a new Focus by clicking the + icon in the lower left corner of the Focus Preference box.

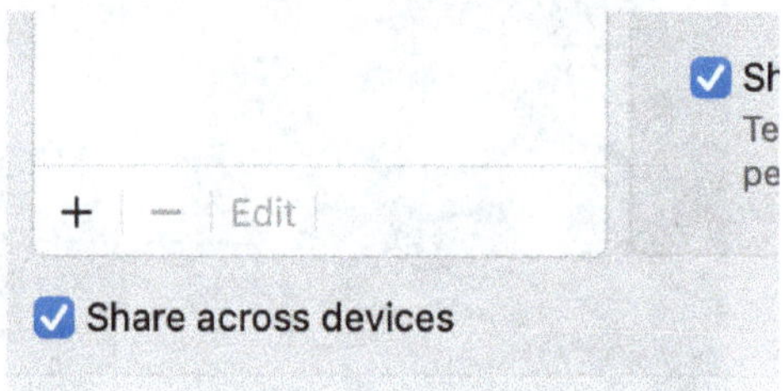

Click the custom option when prompted.

Give your Focus a name, pick the colors, and set an icon, then click the blue Add in the bottom right corner.

It will now be added and you can go in and make any edits to it. It will also be available on any other device you are signed into with iCloud.

Universal Control

Some people like to really invest in the Apple ecosystem—and who can blame them? They make great products. So they might have an iMac, MacBook, and iPad. Apple understands these users and has created a feature called Universal Control. Universal Control lets you share things (from files and images to keyboards and trackpads) easily. What does that mean? Let's pretend you have a MacBook and iPad mini. When enabled, you can open Pages on your iPad, and drag an image from your MacBook to your iPad mini. You can also share your MacBook's trackpad and keyboard with your iPad.

Using it is pretty simple. Put your iPad next to your MacBook and make sure they are on the same wireless network and have Bluetooth on—or connect the iPad to the MacBook with a USB-C, then drag your mouse to the edge of the screen to move it onto your iPad screen. It's all pretty intuitive. Both devices also need to be running the latest version of MacOS (OS Ventura) and iPadOS (OS15). If you are reading this book at the publication date, that's bad news for you because MacOS Ventura is not quite out as of this writing. It also might not launch with the first OS update. It is expected in the fall.

If you want to prepare for it, then you just need to set up a couple of things. First, on your MacBook or iMac, go to the Apple Menu in the upper left corner, then select System Preference, and finally go to General. In the General menu, check off Allow Handoff between this Mac and your iCloud devices. Next, on your iPad, go to the Settings app, then General; next, turn on AirPlay & Handoff if it is toggled off.

Shortcuts

Shortcuts has been a popular mobile app; it's now available on Mac. It allows you to create automated tasks to help you get more work done. You can find the Shortcut app in the Launchpad.

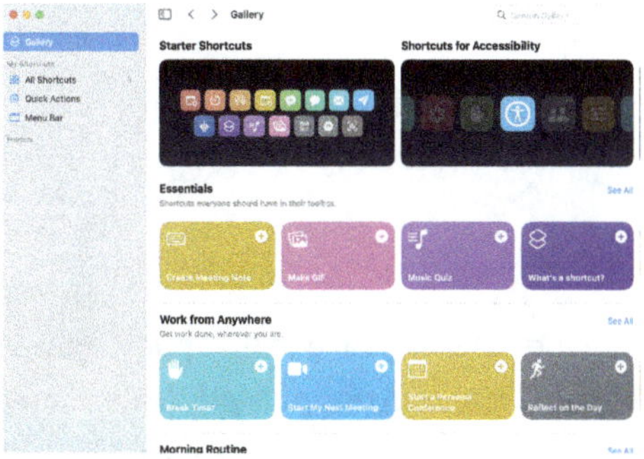

Live Text (Photos)

Photos become smarter in Ventura. You can now do more than stare at your gorgeous face! You can pull information from the photo! What do I mean by that? Let's say take a look at a picture of one of my dogs as a puppy. Adorable, right?! But what kind of dog is she?

With Live photos you can find out! Go to the top bar, then click the "i" icon with the stars on it.

If there's something in that photo that Live photo picks up on, then you'll see a small icon hovering over the photo. In this case there's a little paw print. That should tell you that it thinks this is some sort of animal.

When I click on the icon, it brings up a popup that tells me, that's not only a dog—that's a Jack Russell Terrier; it then has information about the breed.

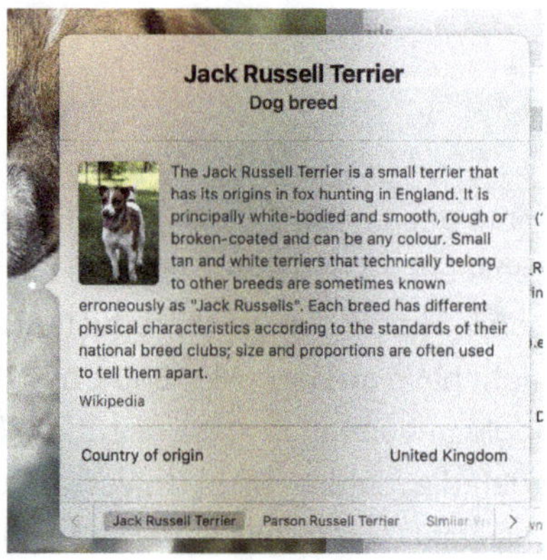

It's not just dogs this kind of look up works on. It works on landmarks, and other things as well.

In the photo below of an audiobook, it will show the name of the book, the author (hey, look! It's my pen name!), a description, and where to buy it.

That's pretty smart, right? But it gets smarter! It also recognizes text. You can highlight words in a photo the same way you would anywhere else—just drag your mouse over it! So if you have a book cover, like in the example below, you don't have to type the name to look it up. You can just highlight it, and copy and paste it! Just right click and select Copy from the menu (or press Command+C on your keyboard).

Maps

Maps got a small upgrade Ventura, but it still functions largely the same.

The biggest difference with the Ventura update is buildings now have more shape. So, in the example below of an amusement park, you can see the shape of the castle and mountain. This is only available in some regions.

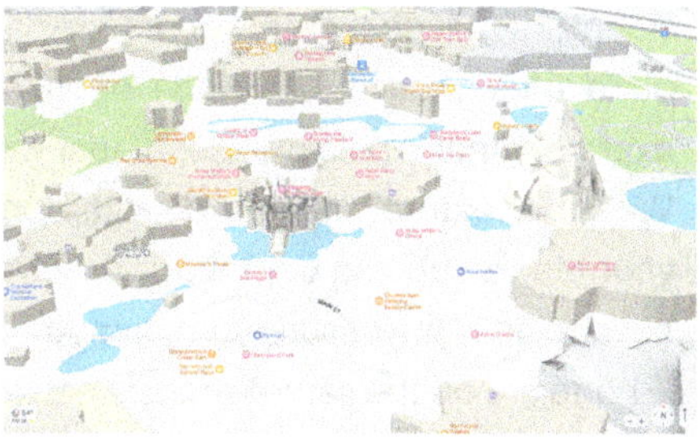

Some, but not all, cities also have more in terms of lanes on the road; if the city has been configured, you'll be able to see more details on lanes to help you navigate through the city and know what lanes to be in. If you don't see this detail, it's because the city has not been set up yet.

Continuity Camera

One of the things I love most about the Apple ecosystem is how well devices work with each other; that is becoming more and more true with each OS update.

The MacBook has a pretty decent webcam. But you know what has an even better webcam? Your iPhone! Think about that stunning camera lens on the back of your camera being able to capture you. Suddenly, your conferences went from HD to 4K! What's even nicer is now, Center Stage is on the iPhone—that means the camera stays focused on you as you move around.

A feature that cool probably requires a huge amount of setup, right? Nope! You ever hear that Apple phrase, "It just works"? Well, this feature...it just works! (as long as your Mac is running OS Ventura) All you have to do is make sure your computer and iPhone are on the same wireless network.

Let me show you how it works in Zoom. Here's how I look on my MacBook without my iPhone:

Not bad. But now I go to the video tab in Zoom and select my iPhone as the camera. You should see any available webcam listed. One will be the name of your iPhone followed by "Camera"; that's the one you want.

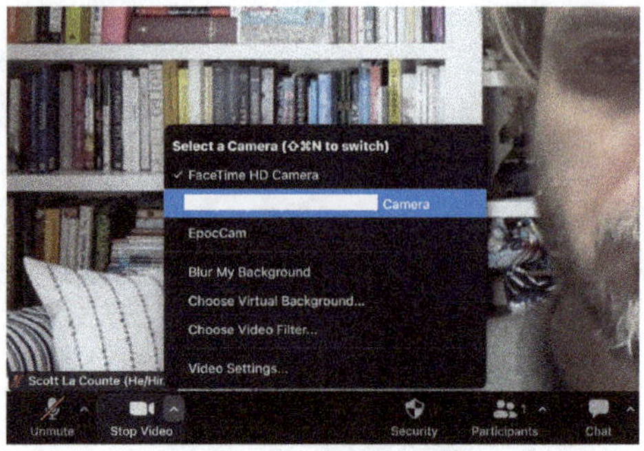

You'll hear a little bell-type noise, then after a second or two, your iPhone's camera will appear.

The difference is pretty crazy; my office doesn't have great lighting, but when I switch to my iPhone for meetings, the image not only looks clearer, the lighting looks flawless.

The example above is Zoom, but the feature works on most video conference apps (FaceTime, Microsoft Teams, etc.).

There are all kinds of ways to mount a camera to make this happen, but the way Apple has promoted is with the Belkin mount, which is $29.99 and called "iPhone Mount with MagSafe for Mac Notebooks".

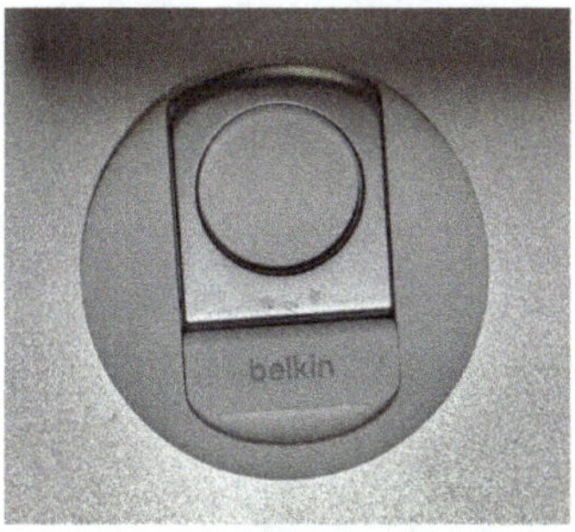

It's very small and clips easily to the back of your phone, and then slips on your MacBook.

Chapter 7: Using Mac Apps

Now that you know about how Mac works (and how to find cat memes), I'm going to talk about the pre-installed programs.

Phone Calls

Apple products really work best with other Apple products; that's even truer with Catalina, where you can sync your iPhone account to make phone calls (both video and regular) and send messages right from your Mac. Additionally, you can even use your iPhone's data connection to get the Internet on your laptop on the go—this is especially handy while travelling if you don't want to pay for Wi-Fi spots that charge for access (just keep in mind that your data connection does have monthly limits and using a computer can go through those limits very quickly—in other words, this probably isn't something you want to do to stream Netflix movies).

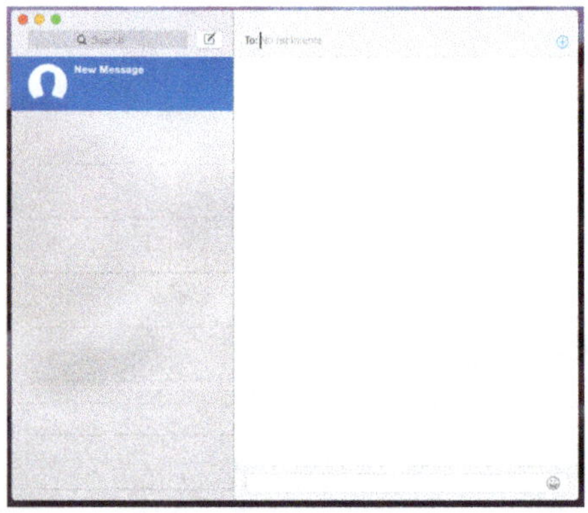

Contacts

Unless you are a business person, having contacts on your computer might not seem necessary; here's the advantage of it—it syncs with your phone. So having a contact on your computer will carry over to your other mobile devices. To use it, go to your Launchpad, then click the icon.

If you're signed into iCloud, then you should see dozens of contacts already. To create a new contact, click on the (+) button at the bottom of the main window. On the next screen add all the info you want—it can be as much or as little as you desire. Some contacts may only need a website address, others might have mailing address—it's entirely up to you how much information you add. You can also edit a contact by finding their name, then clicking on the Edit button. If you want to delete someone, then find their name and hit Delete on your keyboard (you can also delete by clicking on their name with two fingers).

Message

When you use Messages from your Mac to send messages just keep in mind that it's kind of like instant messaging for Mac users —that means it's designed to work with Mac products...nothing else.

Setting Up Message

To set up Message, click the Messages icon to launch it.

If you were already logged into iCloud on the Mac, you will automatically be logged into Message.

If you'd like to change this account or haven't yet logged in, select Messages > Preferences on the top menu bar.

When the Accounts dialogue box comes up, click on the Accounts tab.

In the left-hand window, you will see Message. Select it.

The following screen will prompt you to enter the email address and password associated with iCloud. Do so and click the blue Sign In button to complete the setup process.

Setting Up Other IM Clients

While Message is made for Mac products, you can use it for other messaging services like Google, Yahoo, and AOL.

To add other instant messaging (IM) clients to Messages:

1. Open up Messages if it isn't already running.
2. On the top menu bar, click Messages > Add Account.

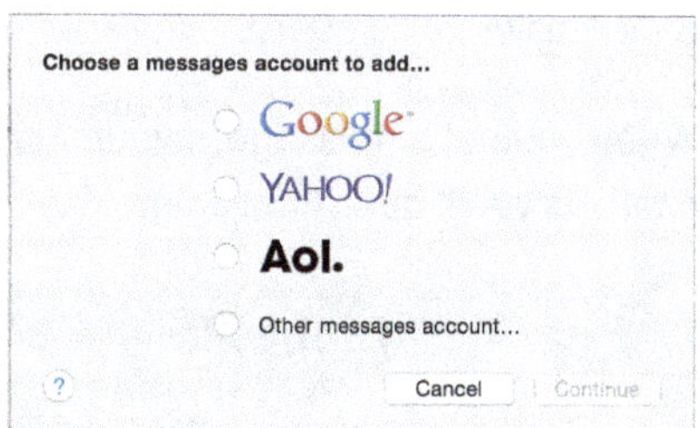

3. Select the type of account that you'd like to add, such as Gmail or Yahoo, and select Continue.

4. You will be prompted to enter the appropriate email address and password, and click the Set Up button to finish.

So now that it's set up, how do you send a message?

Start New Conversation

Before we begin, take a look at the entire Messages screen. It should be totally empty with no conversations. On the left sidebar it will say No Conversations. This is where you will be able to change between different conversations with people by clicking on each one. On the right-hand side, you will also see No Conversation Selected. Here is where you will be able to type new messages and read everything in whatever conversation is currently selected. If you have an iPhone (or any phone for that matter), it will be like the screen where you read your text messages.

To create a new conversation with someone, click the Compose new message button located at the top of the left sidebar, next to the search bar. It should look a little pencil inside of a square.

When you get a message, if your sound is enabled, you'll get a little chime.

Tapbacks

If you've used Stickers on the iPad and iPhone, you might be disappointed to see that feature has not yet arrived on MacOS. There is one feature from iOS: Tapbacks. Tapbacks let you respond to a message to indicate you like what the message says or that you agree with it. To use it, right-click (two-finger click) on any message and select your response.

Pinning Messages

If you text a lot, then it might get a little cumbersome replying. The way Messages works is the most recent conversations go to the top. This mostly works well, but you can also pin favorites to the top.

In the example below, my wife is pinned to the top of the conversations. Even though other people have written to me more recently, she will always be up there (unless I remove her). That makes it easy to reply.

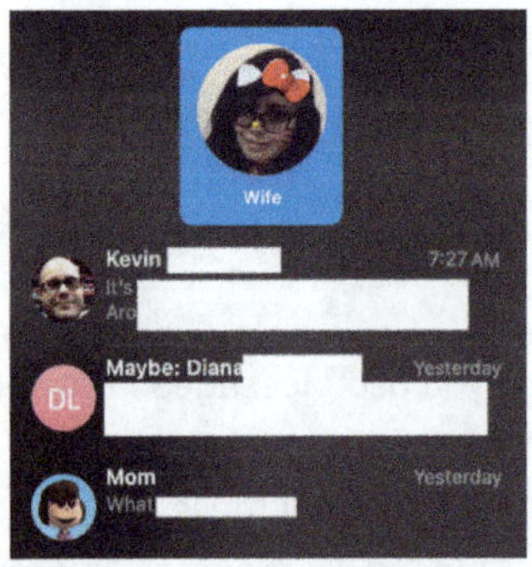

To add or remove someone from the top, drag / swipe with your mouse over the message, then tap the pin.

If you want to remove them, right click the message, and select unpin.

You can have several people pinned to the top. Personally, I find three is good, but you can add even more.

Message Tagging

If you have used messaging programs like Slack, then you are probably all too familiar with tagging someone in a conversation. Tagging gets the person's attention and starts a new thread within the conversation.

So if you are in a large text message exchange, then when you tag someone, everyone can read it, but everyone is not notified. So it's a little less obtrusive.

To tag someone in a conversation, just put an @ in front of their name when you reply.

Replying to Messages

Obviously, you can reply to a message by typing the message in the box and pressing return on your keyboard. But that only replies to the last message. What if the message is several threads up? Or what if it's a group and you want to reply to one particular message from a specific person?

To reply to a message that's higher up, right click over that message, and then select reply.

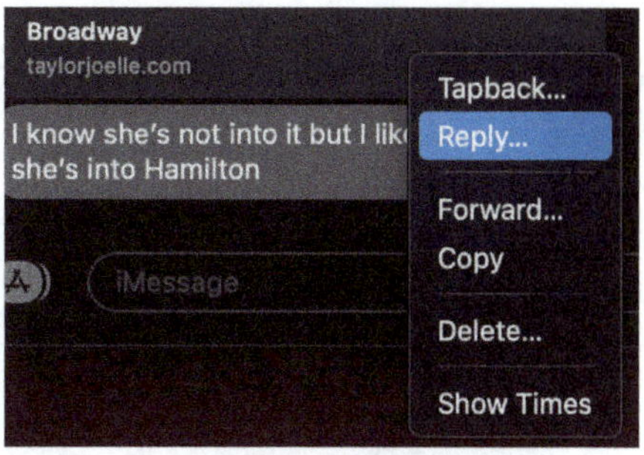

When you do this, the message will show up with a reply underneath it.

It will also show up as the last message sent but with an arrow notifying the user that you've replied to something in particular.

Sending Photos

When you send groups of photos, Messages will lay out photos of less than three vertically. Tap them to make them bigger.

If you send more than three photos, then they'll stack on top of each other, and you swipe through them.

Edit and Unsend messages

Did you make a typo in a message? Or maybe you regret sending it all together. You can unsend a message and edit it… kind of. There's some important caveats here. One, it must be a message you have recently sent—not one from several hours ago. Two, the person on the other end of the message needs to have the current OS running. Three, the other person also gets notified that the message was either unsent or edited. So don't think you can tell the person you never said that.

To use it, right click on the message, then select the option that you want. If you don't see the option, then too much time has passed.

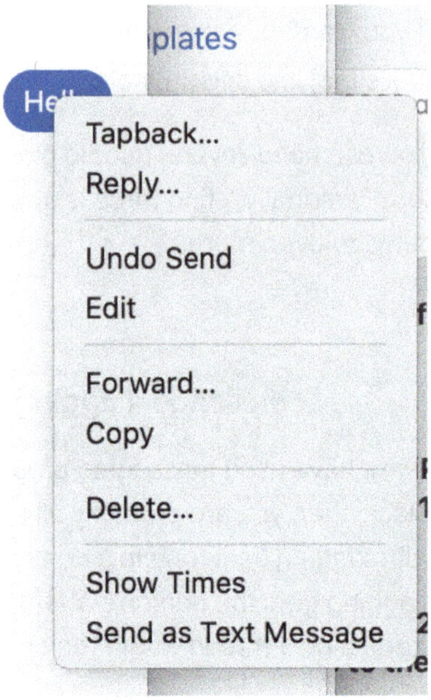

FaceTime

FaceTime allows you to connect with friends and family using your computer's built-in camera. I've heard people say they are so worried that someone is watching them through their webcam that they cover it with tape. When FaceTime is in use (i.e. when the camera is on and people can see you) a bright green light comes on—so you don't have to worry about people spying on you…if you don't see the light, then the camera is off.

The app can be launched by clicking on Launchpad > FaceTime.

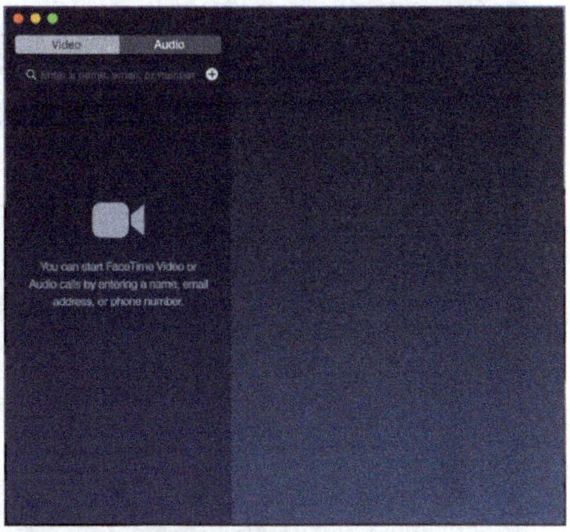

On the left side you can enter a person's name if they are in your Contacts, or a phone number. For FaceTime to work, the other person must also have an Apple device, and accept your call.

You can also use FaceTime audio. This lets you call someone without the camera—it's essentially a Wi-Fi phone call.

Using FaceTime to Keep Family Together

How do you keep people together when they are apart? This is something Apple has thought deeply about. FaceTime on the Mac looks better than ever. Later in fall 2021, you will be able to watch movies together, listen to music together, and even troubleshoot device problems by sharing your device screen. It's called SharePlay. Unfortunately, some of these features are coming later in the fall, so this instructional guide cannot include them at this writing.

To get started, open the FaceTime app from your launchpad.

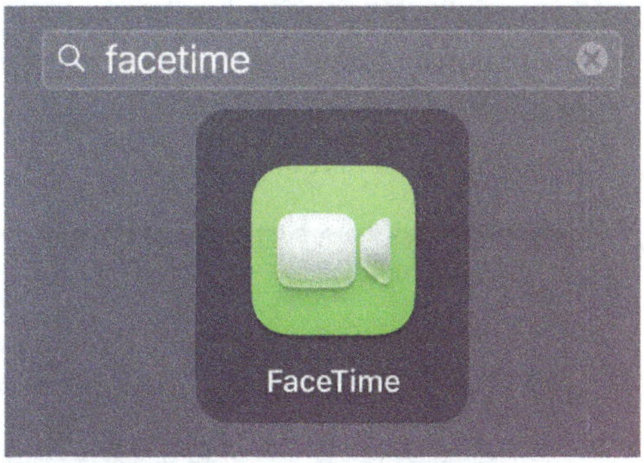

You have two options: Create Link or New FaceTime Call. Creating a link will let someone who doesn't have a Mac or Apple device join in on the call.

The Create Link button will give you a sharable link that you can give out to people. So they can open it inside Chrome on a Windows computer. Just tap the copy button and paste it wherever you want people to see it. You can also tap Add Name to give it a name.

If you prefer to call someone directly, then tap the green New FaceTime button and type in their name.

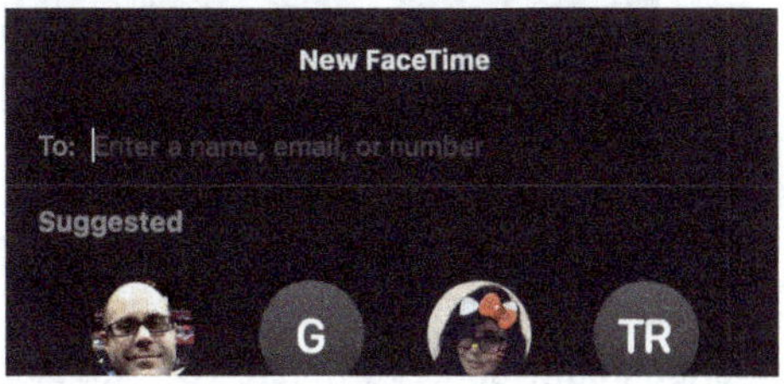

Your preview box is in the lower corner, but it can be moved anywhere on the screen by tapping and holding it, then dragging.

If you make this preview box larger, there's one option available to you. On the bottom center is a small image icon; tap that and it will blur or unblur your background.

If you use FaceTime on your iPhone or iPad, then you'll notice several options are missing—such as adding effects. Mac does not support those as of this writing.

Over in the bottom left corner there's a few other options—the first is the left pane hide / show icon; this reveals a left sidebar where you have access to admitting people into the video call. Next to that is the mic (click to mute yourself), video (click to turn your video off), and X to leave call.

If someone joins your call, then click the left pane icon, then click the green checkmark icon. From here you can also add people and grab the link one more time to share it.

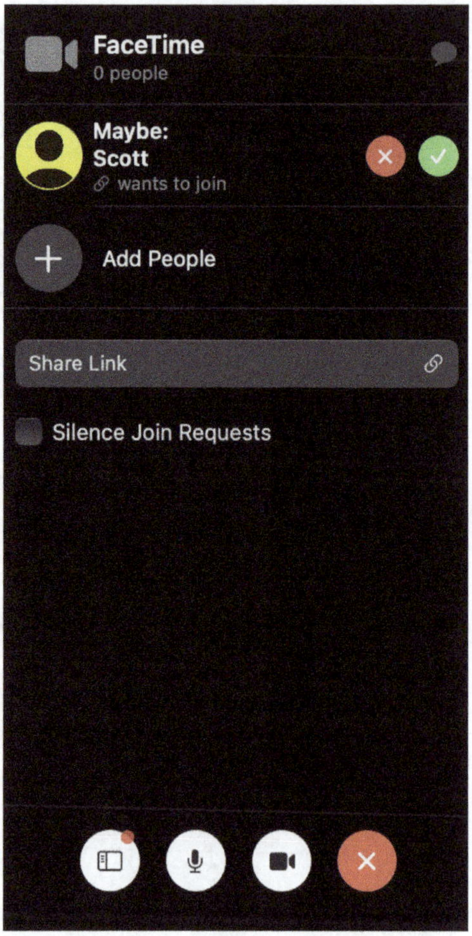

Calendar

Calendar is another feature that can be synced to your iCloud account—so as long as you're using the same account, then everything you put in your calendar from your computer will also show up on your iPhone and iPad. You can also sync the calendar to other ones you may be using online like Google or Yahoo.

To get started with it, go to your Launchpad in the Dock and click on the Calendar icon.

At the top of the application window from left to right you have the standard stoplight buttons, Calendars, New Event (+), several different views including Day and Month, and the Search bar.

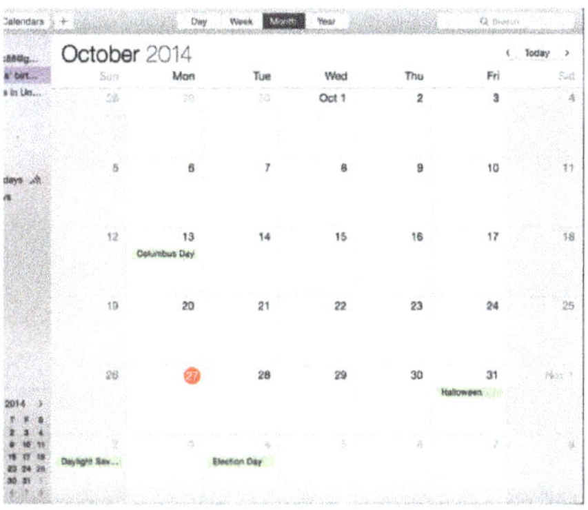

Syncing Calendars

If you already use a calendar with iCloud, Google, Yahoo, or any other provider, you can sync it up with the Mac Calendar application.

In the top menu bar click Calendar > Add Account.

Like you did with Mail, you'll be prompted to enter your name, email address, and password.

Once you finish the setup process your events from that calendar should automatically populate in the Calendar window. If you have multiple accounts with separate calendars, you can filter through them by clicking on the Calendars button in the toolbar, and checking or unchecking the boxes next to the appropriate calendars.

Changing Views

You can change the calendar view between Day, Week, Month, or Year by clicking on the corresponding button in the toolbar.

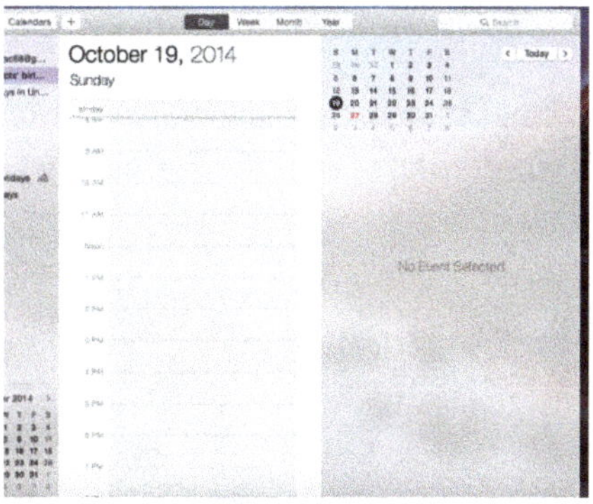

Day will display all of that day's events, broken down by hour.

Week will show you the whole week at a glance, and displays blocks for events so you can easily see when you have events, and if you have any upcoming free time.

The Month view will probably be your default view if you just need your calendar to remind you about bill payments and due dates, or don't have too many appointments each month but they are scattered through the month.

Reminders

As the name implies, the Reminders application is used to remind you of things—and, as you might have guessed by now, it can be synced using iCloud to the Reminders app on your iPhone or iPad.

The app lets you create lists for things like groceries or anything else on your mind; you can also use the app to schedule when things are due—like paying a bill by the 15th of the month. It can even be set to remind you every time you leave or arrive at your home to turn your home alarm on or off.

You can create shared lists so others in your network can also add things to the list.

To get started, open the app by clicking on the Launchpad icon, then selecting it from the list of apps.

Creating a list is still very simple. Tap Add List from the lower right corner of your screen.

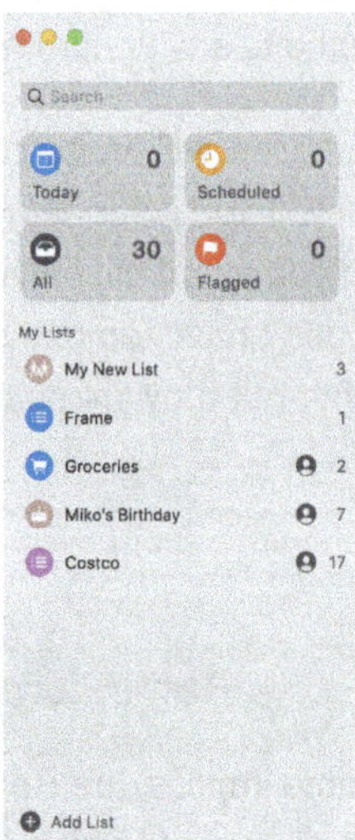

Once you create your first list, you can start adding to it by tapping the '+' button in the upper right corner. This lets you add the item as well as set when it's due and even include images and attachments.

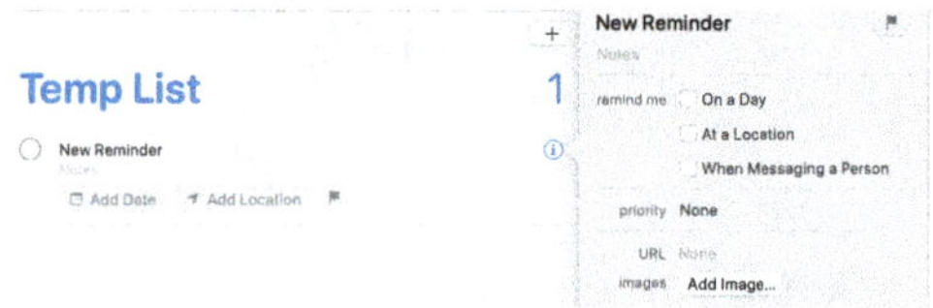

If you tap the i at any point, you'll be able to add more details (such as a due date or even what location to remind you at—you could, for example, have it remind you when you get to the grocery store).

Tap Return on your keyboard to add another item.

To share a list, right-click (two-finger click) the name and add a person that you want to share it with.

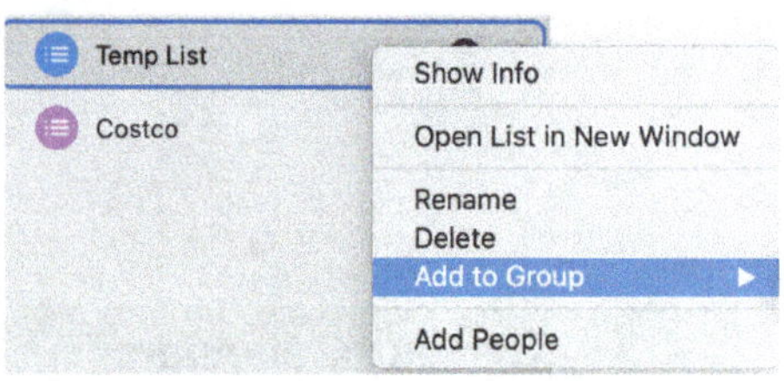

This option also works to remove a list.

MAIL

You may be used to checking your email in your browser. There are a few advantages to emailing through an app. One is instant notifications when mail comes; another is features you might not get in browser-based mail.

If you want to try an app, then there are plenty you can choose from: Airmail, Outlook, Spark, Canary Mail (some are free, some are not).

For this book, I'm going to cover only one app: Apple Mail.

Mail Crash Course

To get started, go to your Launchpad and click the Mail app.

Next, it will ask you to sign into your email provider. The steps vary depending on the services you use, but it will walk you through each step.

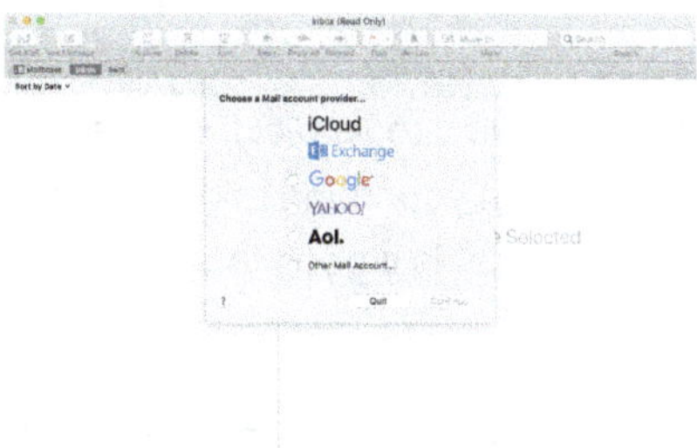

Once you have your mail set up, you'll immediately start seeing your inbox fill up with all the messages from that account. Don't see it? Go to "Get New Mail" under Mailbox in the top menu.

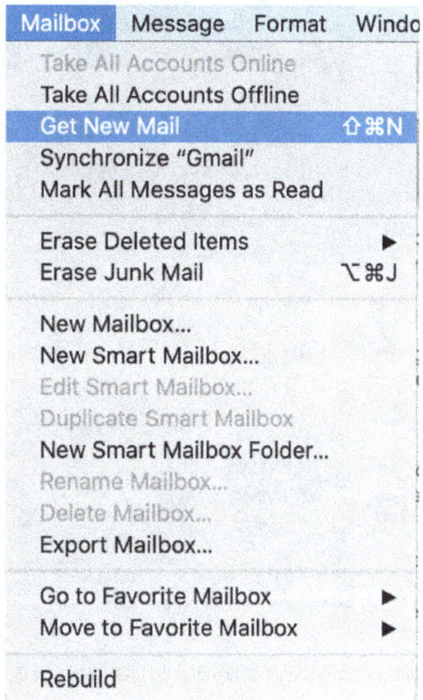

The app should look pretty familiar to you because most the features from your browser mail are there.

A few features you should know about:

Block – If there's someone you don't want to hear from, then block them. To do so, open the email from them, click on their name, and select Block Contact from the dropdown. If only blocking people in real-life was that easy!

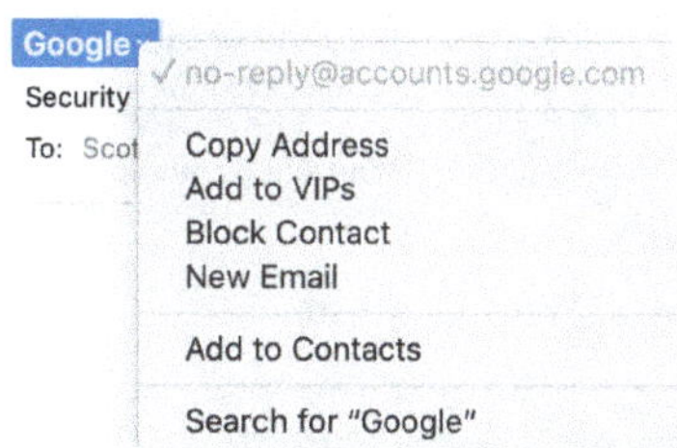

When you right-click (two-finger click) on a mail message, you also have a few options.

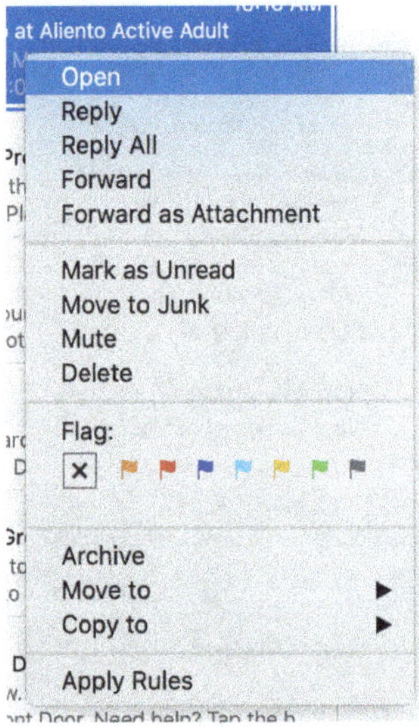

If you have ever used email before, then you will know what Reply, Reply All, etc., do. One that might be new is "Flag." Flag lets you color coordinate different messages to help you find them more easily.

You can also right-click (two-finger click) in the side menu to get more options.

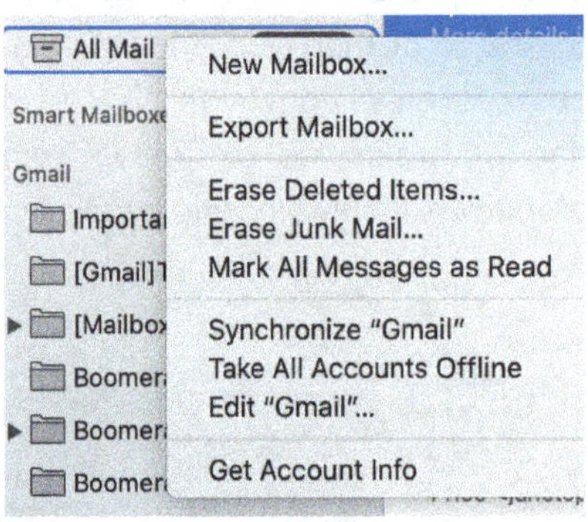

Location Based Reminder

If you want to create a reminder that is location-based (i.e. "when I leave work, remind me to call wife") then follow the steps above.

Click the Information icon next to the reminder (the "i" with a circle).

This will bring up a few extra options. One says, "remind me" with a checkbox for "At a location"; click that checkbox. Next, enter the address, and select if you want the reminder when you get there or when you're leaving there.

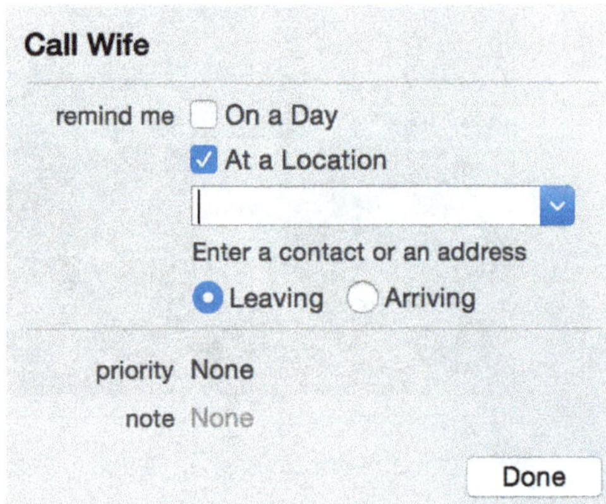

Notes

If you are new to Apple, then the obvious question on your mind might be: why Notes? What is it good for and when should you use it?

Notes is probably not what you want to use to write this year's Christmas Newsletter or create a flier for your lost puppy; Notes really excels when you want to create a shared list, jot down school notes, or do something that doesn't need a lot of formatting.

Notes really shines when you sync it with your iPhone; with your iPhone sync'd, you can write your notes, then use your phone to insert a sketch or image.

Once you have created your Note, you can add it to a folder and everything is searchable, which makes it a very organized way of tracking things.

The Notes Crash Course

To open it, go to the Launchpad icon on your Dock and click the Notes icon.

Notes, like most of the apps in Catalina, syncs to your iPhone and iPad as long as you are logged into the same iCloud account.

Unlike word processing editors that you may be used to, there is no fancy ribbon or menu bar with lots of features. There's a side bar with a list of all your notes (across devices if you use an iPhone / iPad sync'd to your Mac).

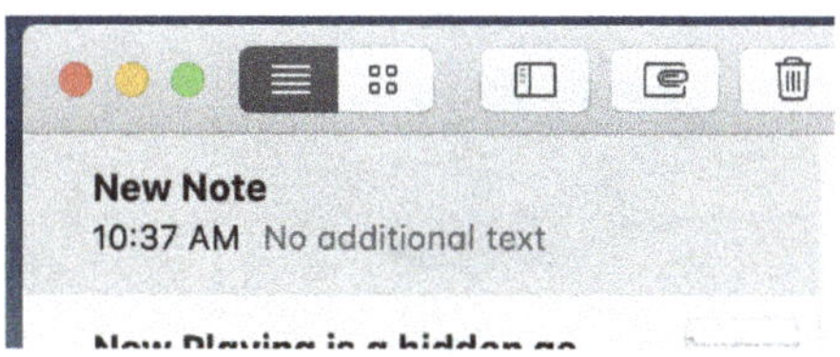

On the top is a very basic menu bar.

Views

The first option next to the app resize options (the red / yellow / green dots) is the view toggle.

This toggle switches between a list view of your notes and a thumbnail view (see below).

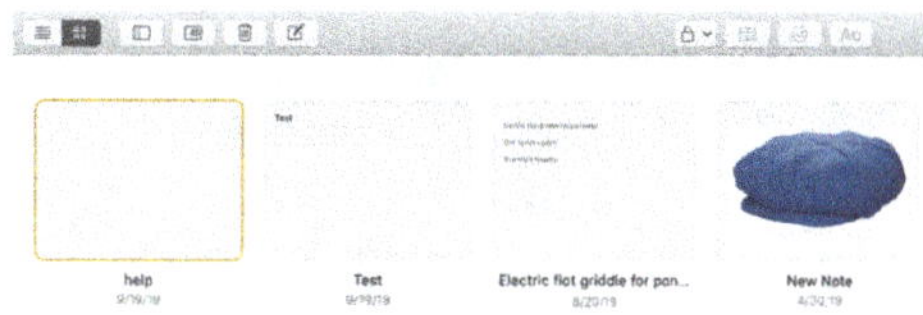

If you are in list view, then you only need to click the Note one time to open it; if you are in thumbnail view, then you will need to double click it.

Folders

The next button is for creating folders.

This brings up a list of all your folders (if any).

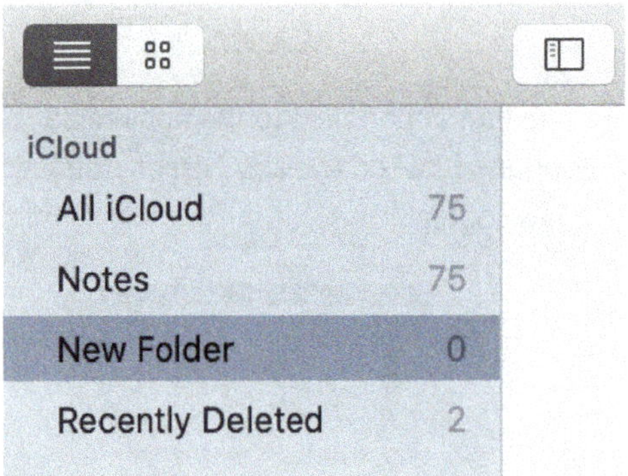

If you don't have one yet, then click New Folder at the bottom of the window.

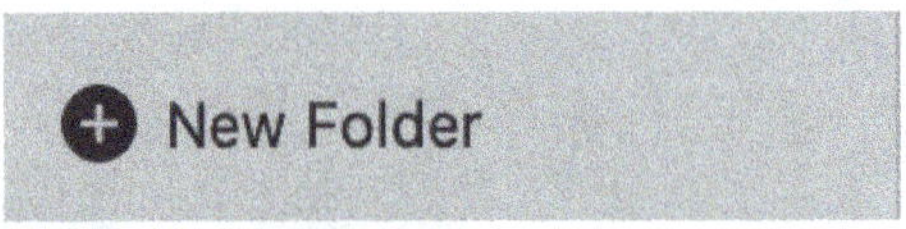

To rename, delete, or add people to the folder, click the three dots with the circle around them.

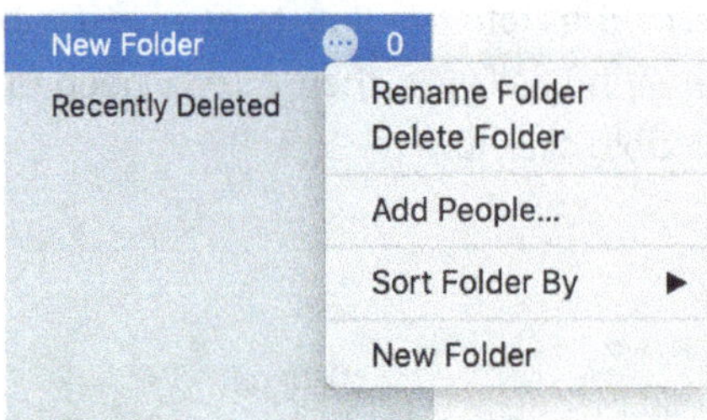

Finally, to add a note to a folder, click it from the side, and then drag it into the desired folder.

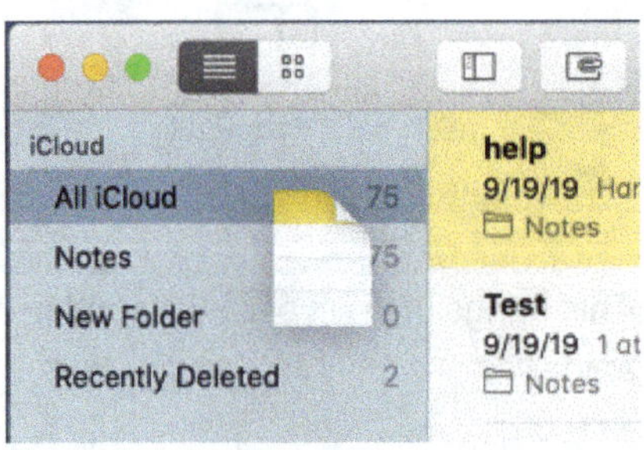

Once you are done, click the view button again to hide the folders panel.

Viewing Attachments

The next option looks like the button to attach things; that's not correct. It's the option to view all the attachments you have added into notes. When you click on it, you can sort by all the different attachment types (Photos & Videos, Scans, Maps, Websites, Audio, and Documents)

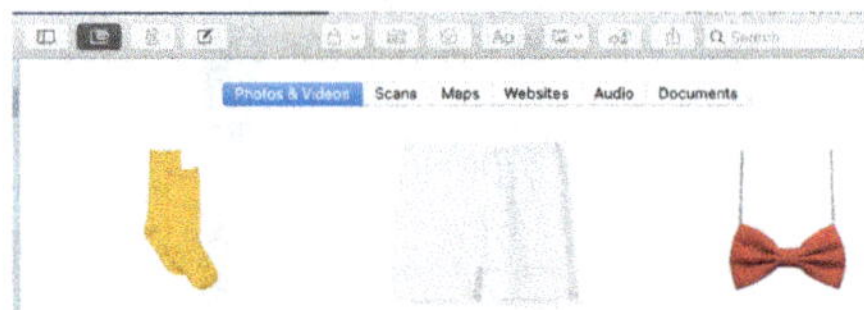

When you double click an attachment, it opens a preview of it (it does not open the note which it's found in). If you would like to see the Note that it is in, then right click to bring up the option menu and click "Show in Note."

Delete Note

The next option is pretty straightforward. It deletes the note that you have currently selected.

Creating a Note

Next to the delete button is the "Create a Note" button, which, as you can expect, creates a note. When you open your note, the left panel will have the name of the note with a time stamp, and the right will have an empty text area to write in. The title of the note will change once you start typing text; the first line of text is the title of your note. You cannot rename the title; if you change the first line of text in the note, then the title is changed automatically.

Lock Note

The security on Notes may not seem quite as robust as other word processors, but there is a very resourceful Lock feature that helps keep private notes secure and for your eyes only. To use it, click the Lock icon.

This will bring up a dialog box that asks you to add a password. Now anytime you want to open the Note, you'll need a password. If you forget your password then you will not be able to access your Note, so be careful!

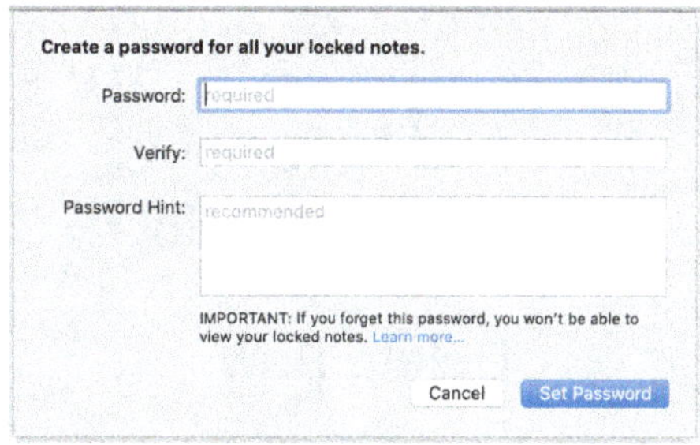

Create a Table

You can also add Tables to your Note. Personally, I would stick to adding tables into other word processing suites, because this is one feature a bit more cumbersome than other tools out there. But if you want to try it out, click the Tables icon.

This adds a very small table to your note—just two rows and two columns.

To add a row or column, click the three little dots on top of the column or to the left of the row, then click what you want to add. You can also delete it using this method.

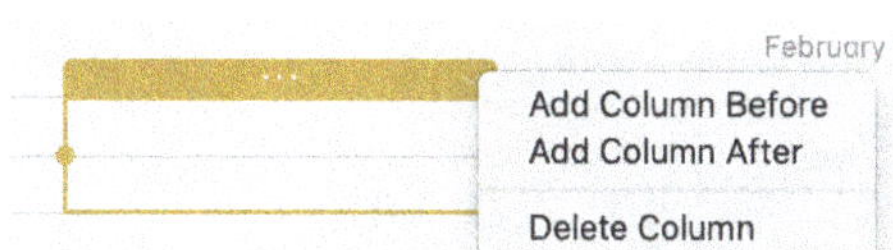

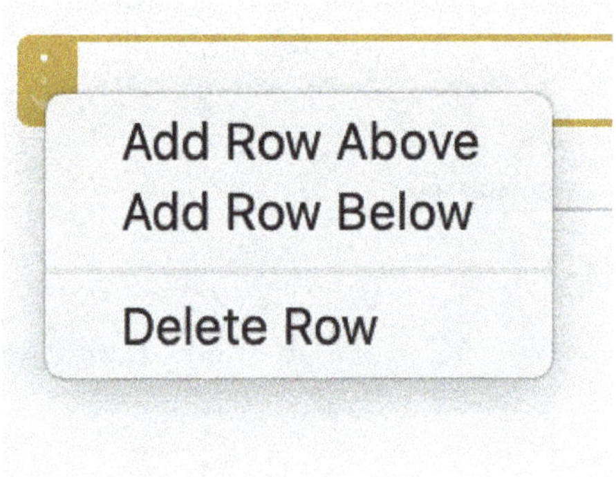

Create a Checklist

If you are using Notes to create a shared list between people (or just a list for yourself), click the Check icon.

This turns each line of text into a list. Hitting return on your keyboard will create a new list item; hitting return twice will take it out of list mode and return it to normal typing.

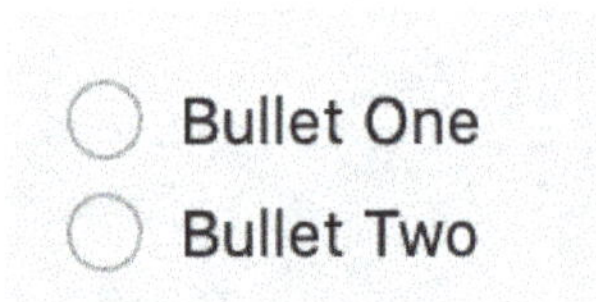

You can click inside any of the circles and check an item off. If you made a mistake, then just uncheck it again.

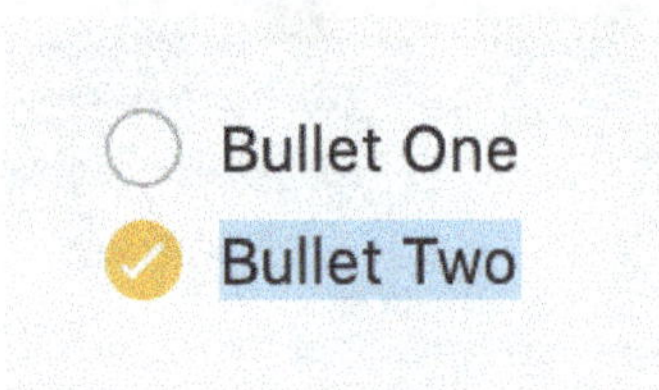

You can also move a list item up or down by right clicking it, then going to "Move List Item."

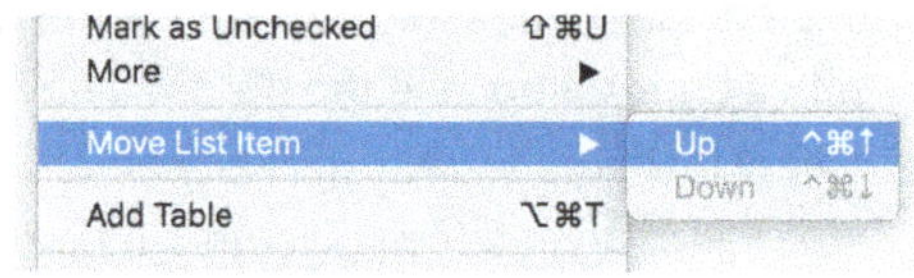

By right clicking, you can also go to More and check off all items (or uncheck all items).

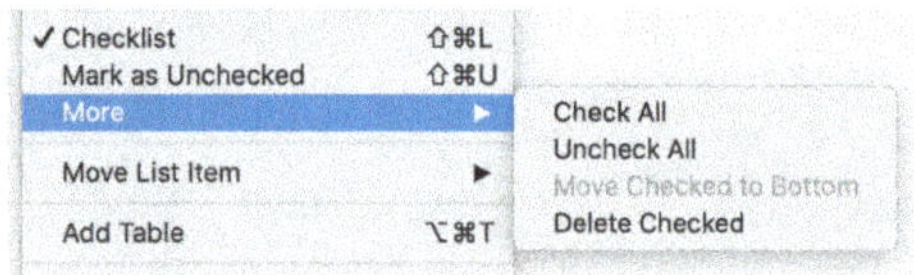

Add a Style

While you can't do as much to the format as you could in other word processors, Notes does have basic styles. To access them, click the Aa icon.

This gives you a drop-down of all the possible styles available.

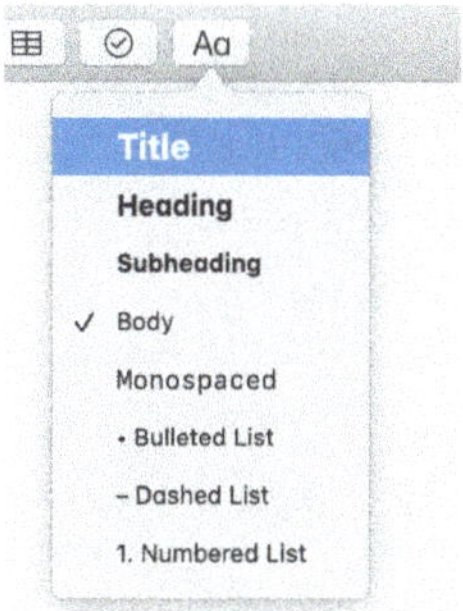

Adding Sketches and Images

One of the many areas Apple has always really shined is with syncing between devices. Using Notes for Mac with your iPhone, you can add in sketches or take photos.

To get started, go to the photos icon. This brings down a drop down of all your options. You can, of course, add any photo on your Mac with the Photos option.

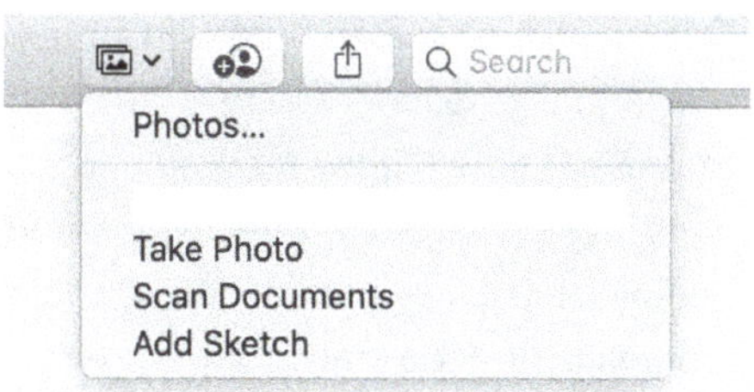

Using the next three options (Take Photo, Scan Documents, Add Sketch) will bring up an image that asks you to connect to your phone to complete the tasks (make sure you are on the same network).

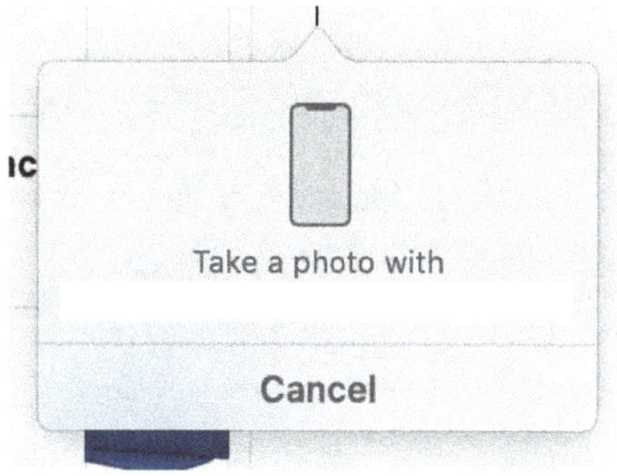

When you add a sketch, you draw it on your phone.

Once you hit done on your phone, it will automatically appear in Notes for Mac.

Adding Collaborators

If you want to add others to your note, click the icon with the person and +.

Next click "Note 'New Note'".

It will ask how you want to add them. Through messages, a link, AirDrop, etc.

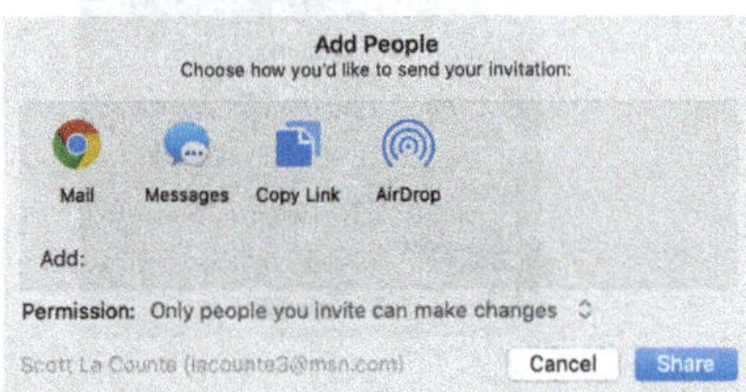

When you're ready, click share, but before you do, click the Permissions drop-down and make sure it's set up the way you want. You can either let the note be view-only for others or you can let them make changes.

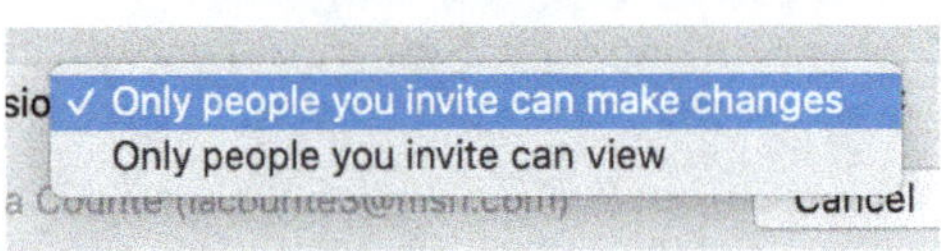

Sharing Notes

If you want to share the note without adding the person to the note, click the share icon.

Next, pick how you would like to share the note.

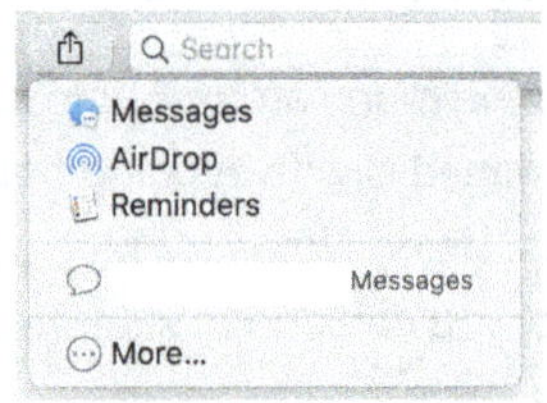

Searching Notes

The last option on the toolbar is the search box. This lets you search all of your notes for different keywords. For example, whenever I go somewhere with a public Wi-Fi, I add the network key to a Wi-Fi password note (I don't recommend this for sensitive passwords); whenever I need to quickly find it, I search for "WiFi" and it comes up immediately.

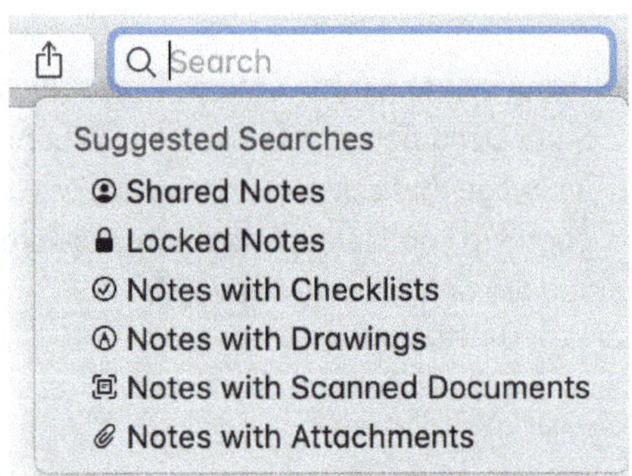

Exporting Notes

Now that we've seen all the features on the toolbar, let's go up one level to the top menu bar. Everything you did in the toolbar, you can also do there; there are also, however, a few extra features.

The first is exporting a Note as a PDF. That's found under File > Export as PDF.

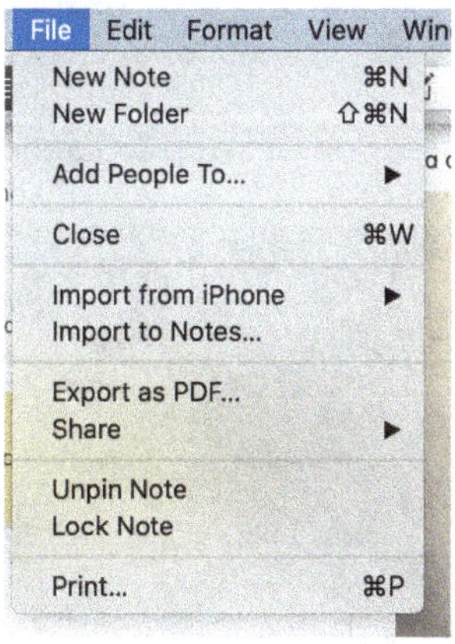

Above Export is the Import option; personally, I find it easier just to share a note from another device, but if you have a copy somewhere and have a reason to import it, then you would go here.

Pinning Notes

Pinning notes is a very basic, but useful feature; when you click on a note and then select to Pin it from File > Pin Note, it sticks it at the top of all your notes to make it easier to find.

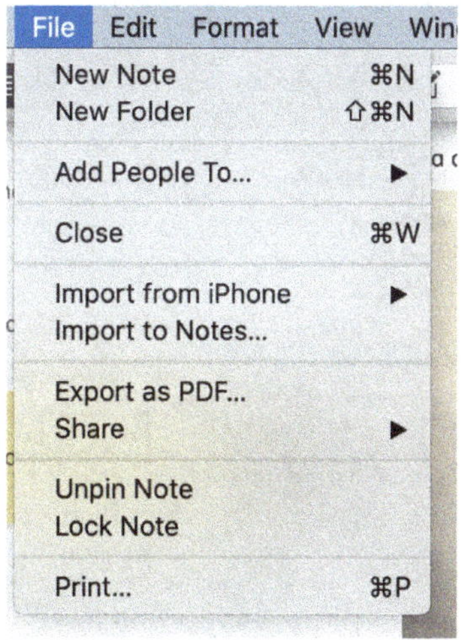

Attaching Files

Unlike many word processing apps, you can actually attach files to Notes. Go to Edit > Attach File.

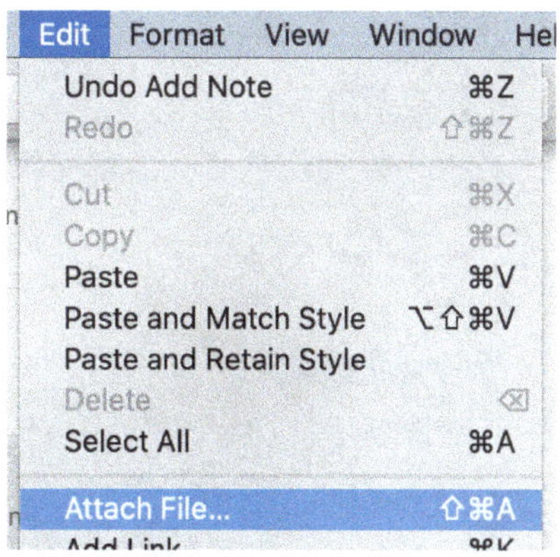

Spell Check

Like any word processing software, there is a spell checker buried in the top menu. You can start spell check by going to Edit > Spelling and Grammar. By default, it checks spelling / grammar as you type.

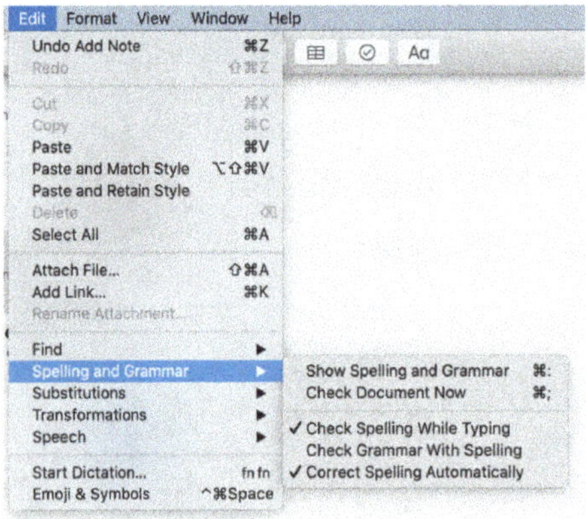

Font Formatter

Finally, while changing the font color / type is not quite as simple as Pages or Word, it is still possible. Go to Format > Font.

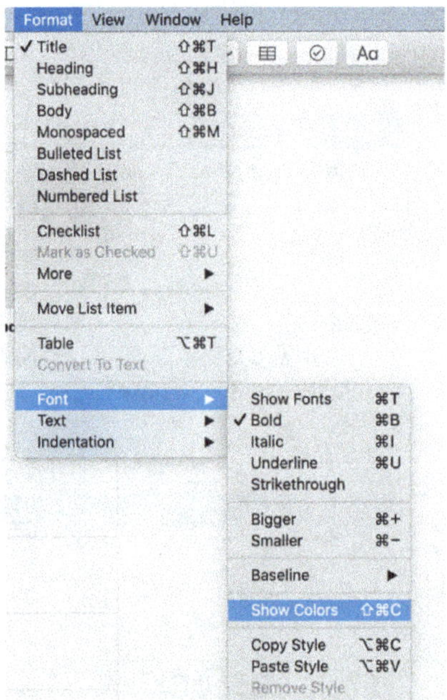

Quick Note

Quick Note lets you quickly jot things down as you work. How does it work? It depends on how you want it to work! To get it to work, you have to first create a shortcut to access it.

Go into LaunchPad and open System Preferences.

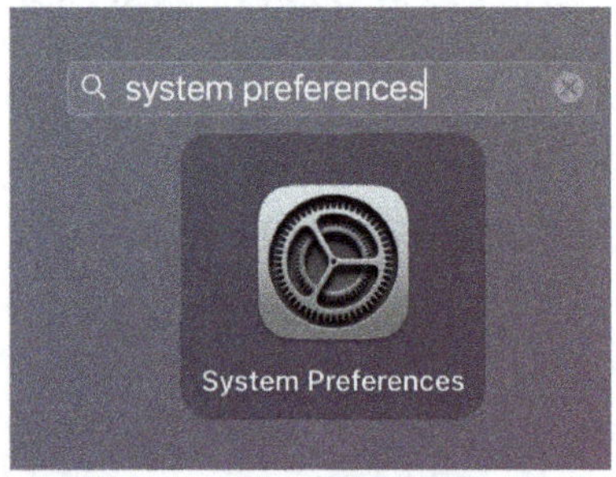

Next, click on Desktop & Screen Saver.

Click the Screen Saver tab.

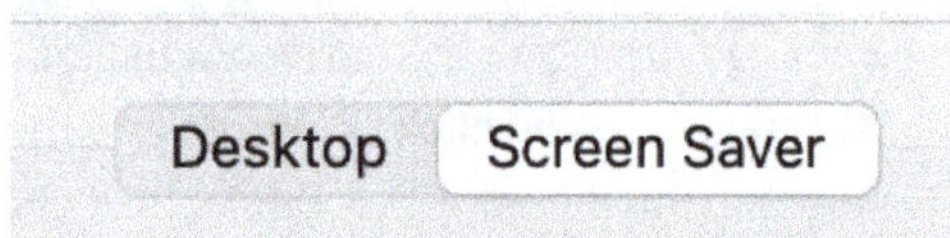

In the lower right corner is a button that says Hot Corners. Click that.

Hot Corners tells the operating system when you go into a corner, you want it to do something. Find a corner, then click the drop-down and select Quick Note.

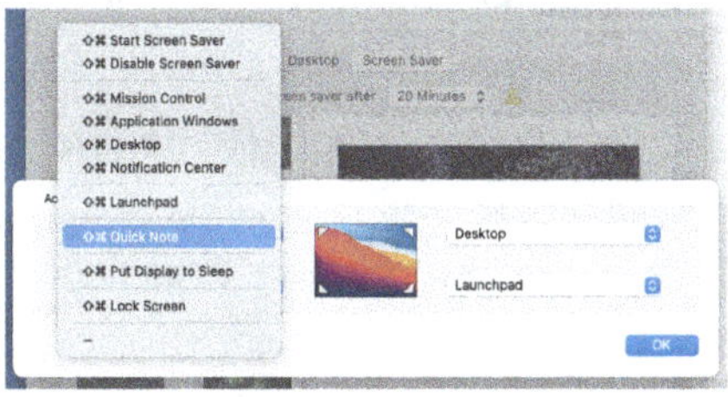

The corner is now activated. I picked the upper left corner. When I move my mouse up there, a tiny box appears. To open the Quick Note, I have to click that box.

Your note should now be opened. It will sync across any device you are signed into with the same iCloud address.

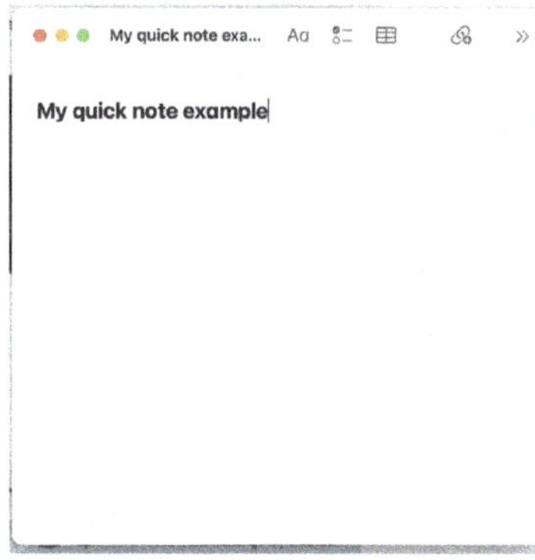

App Store

The App Store is where you'll be able to download and install many different applications that have been developed specifically for use with a Mac computer. These apps will do everything from add new functionalities and make your life easier, to providing a fun way to waste time and play some games during downtime at work. Keep in mind that for the App Store to be functional, you need to be connected to the Internet.

To be clear, apps purchased on the App Store only run on Macs; if you have two Macs, you can download it on both if you have the same account. But you cannot download them on your iPhone or iPad. So, if you are wondering why a game you downloaded on the iPhone or iPad is not available free on your Mac, that's why. Mac apps are developed using an entirely different framework.

Open the App Store by selecting it either through the Dock or Launchpad. The App Store's home page will greet you, showing you the latest and greatest in the world of apps.

At the top you will see different sections: Featured, Top Charts, Categories, Purchases, and Updates.

The Featured, Top Charts, and Categories tabs will show you apps that can be downloaded, but organized in different ways. Featured will show you Best New Apps, Best New Games, Editor's Choices, and collections of different apps that work great together.

Top Charts shows you the best of the best when it comes to available apps, and is broken down by Top Paid, Top Free, and Top Grossing. On the right side, you can also browse through Top Apps broken down by category, in case you wanted to refine your search.

Categories further breaks down your app hunting into different categories like Business, Education, Reference, Productivity, Medical, Entertainment, and Games.

Choosing a category will bring up more selections and the right side will be filled with even more categories. For example, selecting the Business category will bring you to the main Business apps page where the hottest apps are listed. On the right side, smaller categories like Apps for Writers, App Development, or Apps for Designers can be selected. It doesn't matter what category of apps you are currently under; the list remains the same in the right half.

Purchases and Updates are where you can go to view past App Store downloads. The Purchases title can be a bit misleading, because your free apps will also appear here. In the Updates section, you can view which apps need to be updated to the latest version. If you have multiple apps that need updating, you can choose the Update All button and it will go down the entire list.

Photos

Photos has been around on the Mac for quite a while. In OS Catalina, however, it got a bit of a facelift that closer resembles the experience on the iPad and iPhone.

To get started, go to Photos from the Launchpad.

If your Mac is synced to your iPhone, then your photos are synced as well. No need to move them over. If you don't have an iPhone or you have other photos that you'd like to add that weren't taken on an Apple device, then you can go to File > Import.

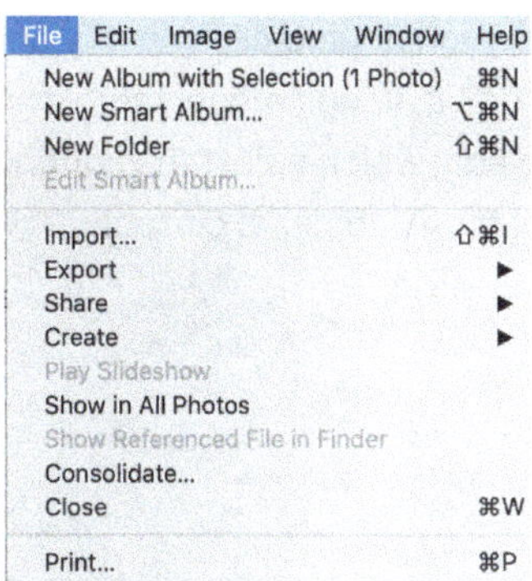

There are a few options to check out in the top menu. The first is the bigger / smaller slider.

This lets you adjust the thumbnail preview size of your photos.

Next to that is the Years / Months / Days / All Photos option, which lets you pick how photos are grouped.

If you have a photo selected, you can click the "i" and see information about the photo (what camera was used, resolution, ISO, file size, and more).

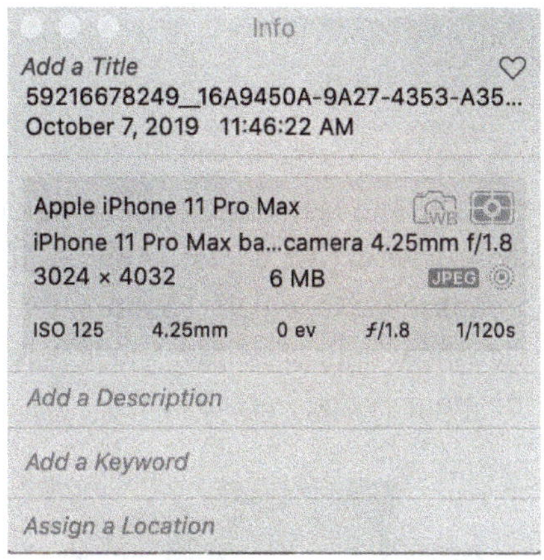

Next to information is the option to share, favorite, rotate, or search for images.

Search is pretty smart—you can search by the names of people or by the location it was taken.

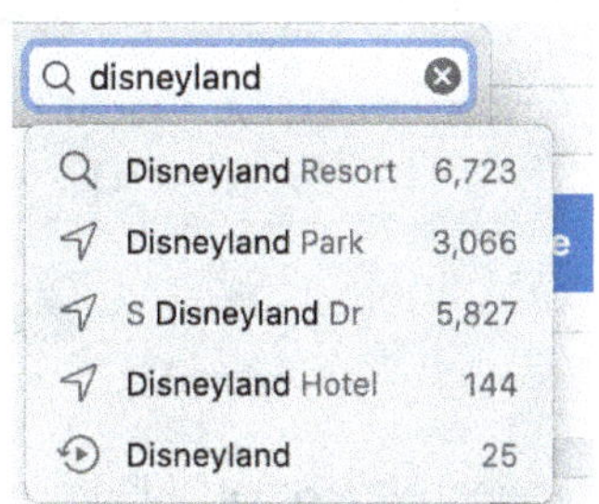

On the left menu, you have the option to view specific photos—photos with people, for example.

If you go into Memories, you can watch slideshows of past photos (Apple's AI groups these together). To watch the slideshow, right-click (two-finger click) on the memory you want to see.

Under Albums in the left menu, you can right-click to create a new Album.

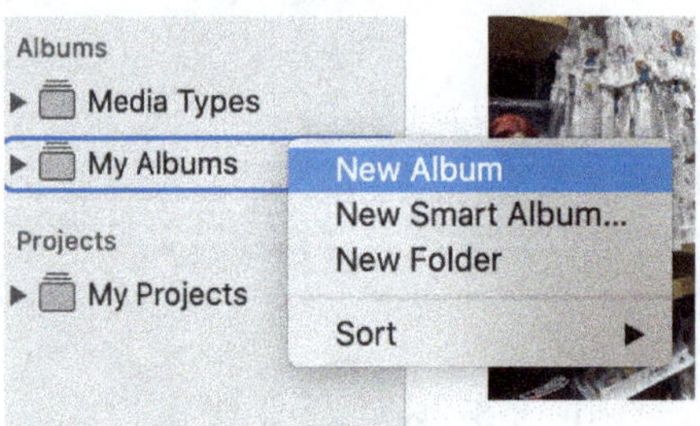

If you select New Smart Album, then you can create an Album based on a defined filter you select.

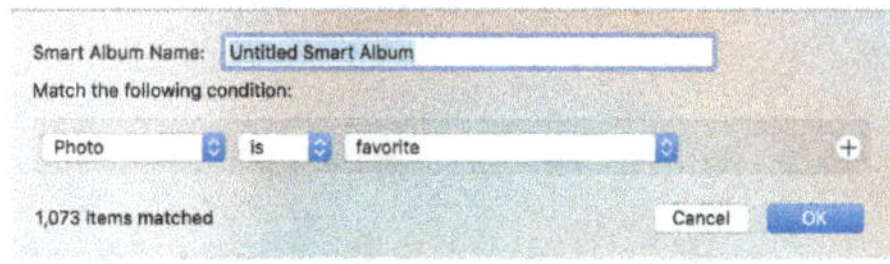

Once you create an Album, then you can right-click on any photo and add it to that Album.

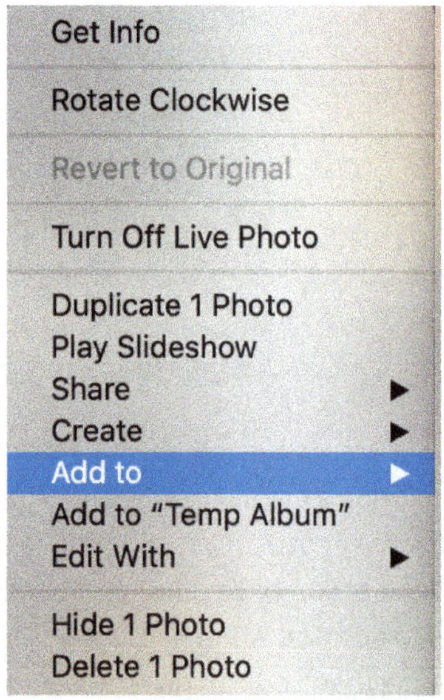

When you double-click on any photo, you can edit it. In edit mode, there's an option to auto edit, which adjust the lighting based on what the AI thinks is correct.

There are dozens of basic and advanced editing options.

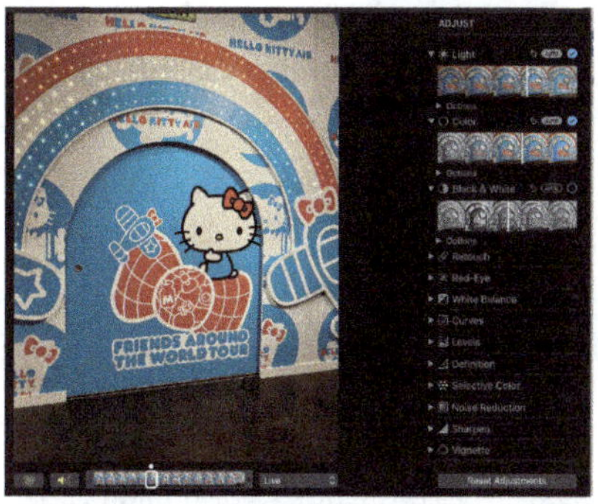

There are three main sections when doing edits (accessible in the top menu): Adjust (lighting corrections), Filters (pre-defined photo filters), and Crop.

Lesser Used Apps

There are a lot of apps on Mac that you probably see but don't use. Here's a rundown of some of those apps and when you might use them.

TextEdit is Apple's answer to Microsoft's Notepad. This is a simple plain-text editor. It's certainly not fancy, but it's good for jotting down notes.

Stickies is a love it or hate it sort of app. If you're in the love it camp, though, they're still there. Stickies are like Post-it notes for your desktop. Just open the Stickies app from Launchpad and start sticking away!

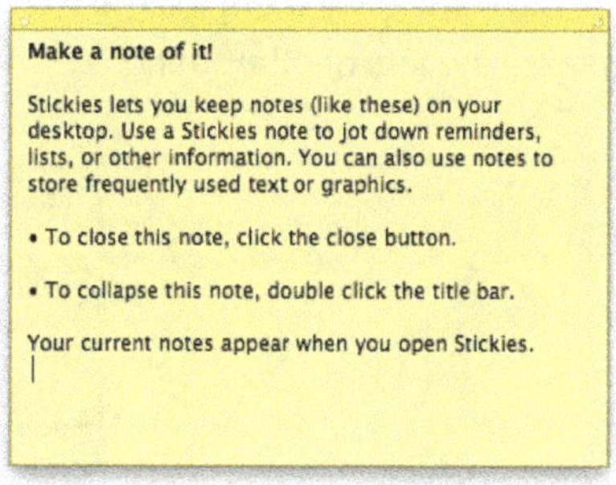

Siri

If you've used Siri on the iPhone, iPad or Apple Watch, then you'll be right at home with this feature. Siri is built into the Dock. To use it, just click the Dock icon.

HINT: There's a shortcut key for bringing up Siri: hold the Command key and Spacebar.

Siri is great for asking general questions, but it also works for doing more involved tasks. Here's a few examples of that:

Drag and Drop Images – Ask Siri to find you photos of something; it will confirm if you want web images or images on your hard drive. It will bring back photos and you can click and drag them into documents, emails, and lots of other things.

Locating Files – Siri works much like the finder…except easier. You can tell Siri to find a specific file, or you can tell Siri to find you all files opened last week, or virtually anything else.

Personal Assistant – Siri is great at doing tasks for you. You can ask Siri to email someone, read text messages, or make an appointment in your calendar. Just ask and see what happens!

If you'd like to change Siri's settings (change the voice from female to male, for example), then go to the Launchpad, open System Preferences, then click Siri.

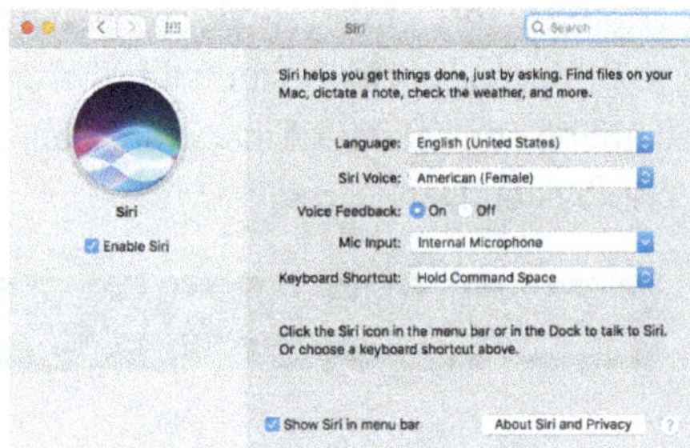

Chapter 8: Apple Services

Introduction

It used to be a few times a year Apple would take the stage and announce something that everyone's head exploded over! The iPhone! The iPad! The Apple Watch! The iPod!

That still happens today, but Apple also is well aware of the reality: most people don't upgrade to new hardware every year. How does a company make money when that happens? In a word: services.

In the past few years (especially in 2019) Apple announced several services—things people would opt into to pay for monthly. It was a way to continue making money even when people were not buying hardware.

For it to work, Apple knew they couldn't just offer a subpar service and expect people to pay because it said Apple. It had to be good. And it is!

iCloud

iCloud is something that Apple doesn't talk a lot about but is perhaps their biggest service. It's estimated that nearly 850 million people use it. The thing about it, however, is many people don't even know they're using it.

What exactly is it? If you are familiar with Google Drive, then the concept is something you probably already understand. It's an online storage locker. But it's more than that. It is a place where you can store files, and it also syncs everything—so if you send a message on your iPhone, it appears on your MacBook and iPad. If you work on a Keynote presentation from your iPad, you can continue where you left off on your iPhone.

What's even better about iCloud is it's affordable. New devices get 5GB for free. From there the price range is as follows (note that these prices may change after printing):

- 50GB: $0.99
- 200GB: $2.99
- 2TB: $9.99

These prices are for everyone in your family. So, if you have five people on your plan, then each person doesn't need their own storage plan. This also means purchases are saved—if one family member buys a book or movie, everyone can access it.

iCloud has become even more powerful as our photo library grows. Photos used to be relatively small, but as cameras have advanced, the size goes up. Most photos on your Mac are several MB big. iCloud means you can keep the newest ones on your phone and put the older ones in the Cloud. It also means you don't have to worry about paying for the phone with the biggest hard drive—in fact, even if you have the biggest hard drive, there's a chance it won't fit all of your photos.

Where Is iCloud?

If you look at your MacBook, you won't see an iCloud app. That's because there isn't an iCloud app. To see iCloud, point your computer browser to iCloud.com.

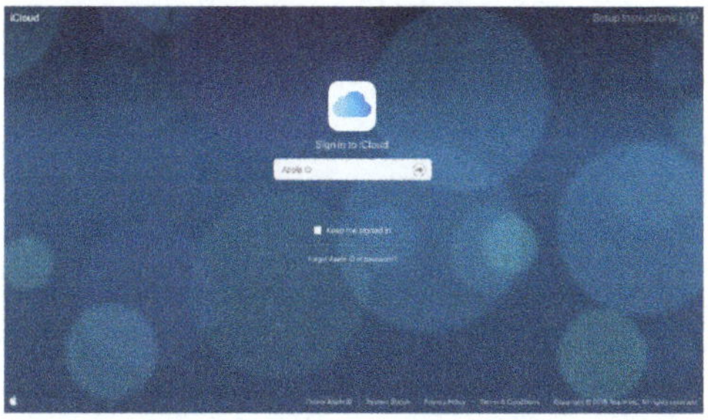

Once you sign in, you'll see all the things stored in your Cloud—photos, contacts, notes, files; these are all things you can access across all of your devices.

In addition, you can use iCloud from any computer (even PCs); this is especially helpful if you need to use Find My Mac, which locates not only your computer, but all of your Apple devices—phones, watches, even AirPods.

Backing Up Your Computer With iCloud

The first thing you should know about iCloud is how to back up your computer with it. This is what you will need to do if you are moving from one Mac to another.

If there's no iCloud app on the computer, then how do you do that? While there is no native app in the traditional sense that you are used to, there are several iCloud settings in System Preferences.

Open the System Preferences; at the top you will see your name and profile picture; click that. That brings up the option to manage iCloud.

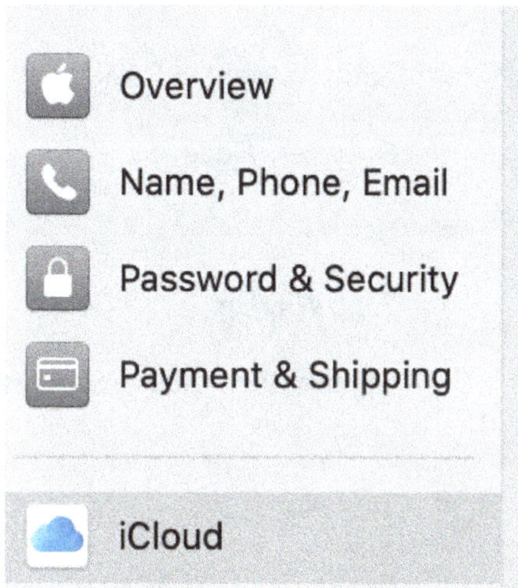

iCloud Drive

To see your cloud files, open the Finder app; on the left menu, there is an option for the iCloud Drive.

You can use iCloud Drive to create and move folders just like you would in the Finder app.

- Greyhound (War)
- Hala (Drama)
- On the Rocks (Drama)

Docuseries

- Becoming You
- Dear…
- Earth At Night In Color
- Greatness Code
- Home
- Long Way Up
- Oprah's Book Club / The Oprah Conversation
- Tiny World
- Visible: Out On Television

Documentary

- Beastie Boys Story
- Boys State
- Dads
- The Elephant Queen

Shows and films are being added monthly, and current shows are getting future seasons, so look for this area to rapidly change.

Apple Music

Apple Music is Apple's music streaming service.

The question most people wonder is which is better: Spotify or Apple Music? On paper it's hard to tell. They both have the same number of songs, and they both cost the same ($9.99 a month, $5 for students, $14.99 for families).

There really is no clear winner. It all comes down to preference. Spotify has some good features—such as an ad-supported free plan.

One of the standout features of Apple Music is iTunes Match. If you are like me and have a large collection of audio files on your computer, then you'll love iTunes Match. Apple puts those files in the Cloud, and you can stream them on any of your devices. This feature is also available if you don't have Apple Music for $25 a year.

Apple Music also plays well with Apple devices; so, if you are an Apple house (i.e. everything you own, from smart speakers to TV media boxes, has the Apple logo), then Apple Music is probably the best one for you.

Apple is compatible with other smart speakers, but it's built to shine on its own devices.

I won't cover Spotify here, but my advice is to try them both (they both have free trials) and see which interface you prefer.

Apple Music Crash Course

Before going over where things are in Apple Music, it's worth noting that Apple

Music can now be accessed from your web browser (in beta form) here: http://beta.music.apple.com.

It's also worth noting that I have a little girl and don't get to listen to a lot of "adult" music, so the examples here are going to show a lot of kid's music!

The main navigation on Apple Music is on the side menu:

- For You
- Browse
- Radio

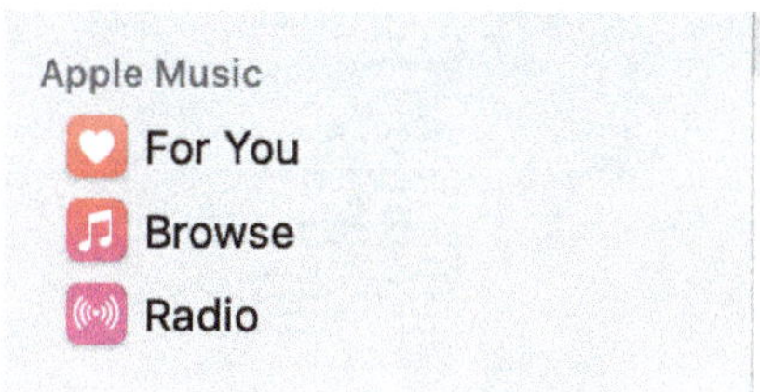

There's also a Library below this of what you have downloaded.

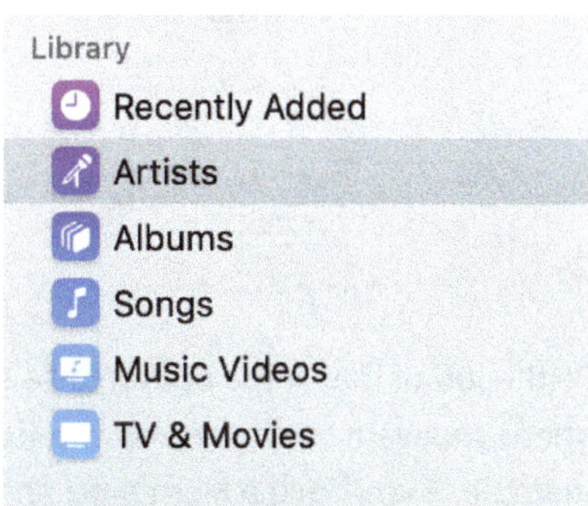

Library

When you create playlists or download songs or albums, this is where you will go to find them.

You can change the categories that show up in this first list by tapping on Edit, then checking off the categories you want. Make sure to hit Done to save your changes.

For You

As you play music, Apple Music starts to get to know you more and more; it makes recommendations based on what you are playing.

In For You, you can get a mix of all these songs and see other recommendations.

In addition to different styles of music, it also has friends' recommendations so you can discover new music based on what your friends are listening to.

Browse

Not digging those recommendations? You can also browse genres in the Browse menu. In addition to different genre categories, you can see what music is new and what music is popular.

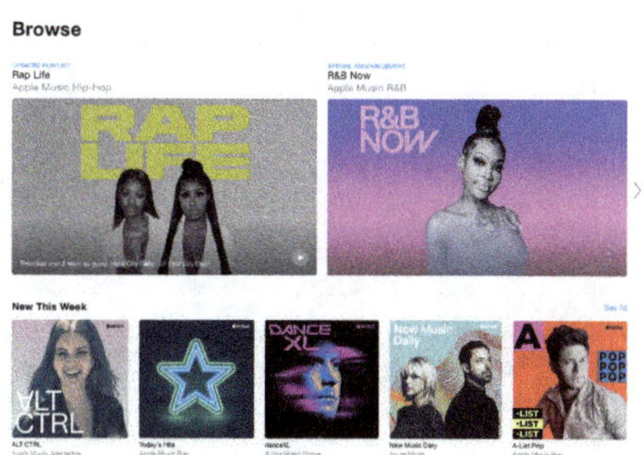

Radio

Radio is Apple's version of AM/FM; the main radio station is Beats One. There are on-air DJs and everything you'd expect from a radio station.

While Beats One is Apple's flagship station, it's not its only station. You can scroll down and tap on Radio Stations under More to explore and see several other stations based on music styles (i.e. country, alternative, rock, etc.). Under this menu, you'll also find a handful of talk stations covering news and sports. Don't expect to find the opinionated talk radio you may listen to on regular radio—it's pretty controversy-free.

Search

The last option is the search menu, which is pretty self-explanatory. Type in what you want to find (i.e. artist, album, genre, etc.).

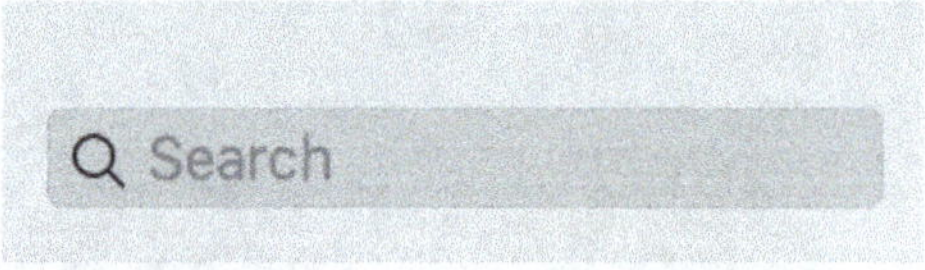

Listening to Music and Creating a Playlist

You can access the music you are currently listening to from the top of your screen.

Right-clicking (two-finger clicking) on the album on this brings up several options. One is to take you to the album, which shows a full screen view.

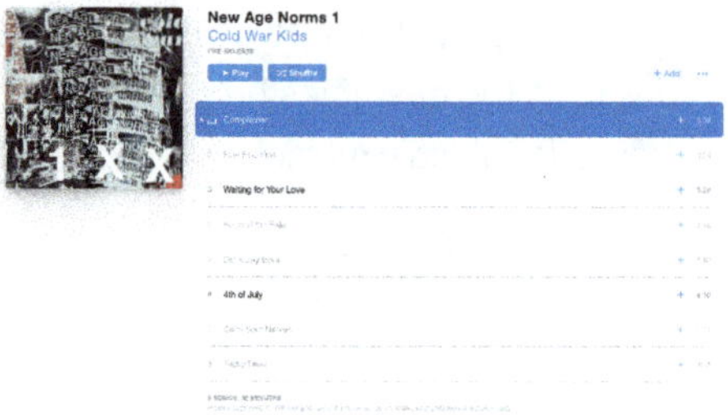

Clicking on the chat-like button will show you the text from what's playing.

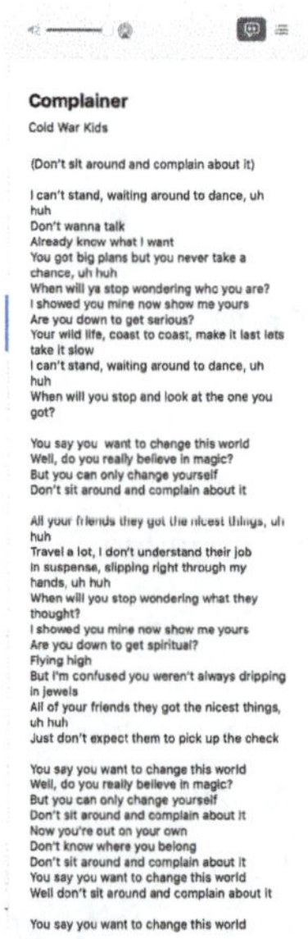

To the left of that is the option to select where you want to play the music. For example, if you have a HomePod and you want to listen wirelessly to the music from that device, you can change it here.

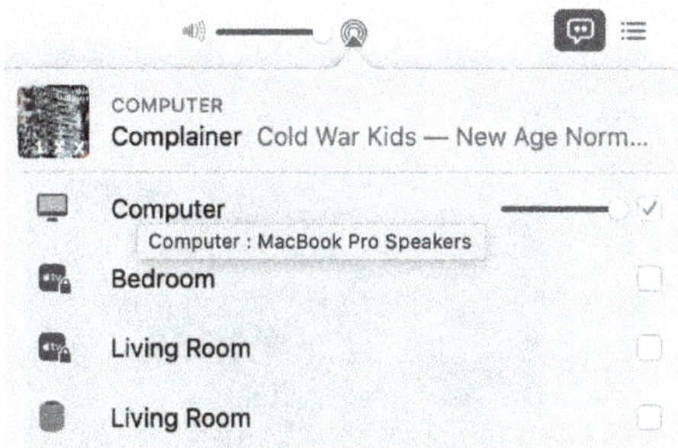

The option on the far right shows the next song(s) in the playlist.

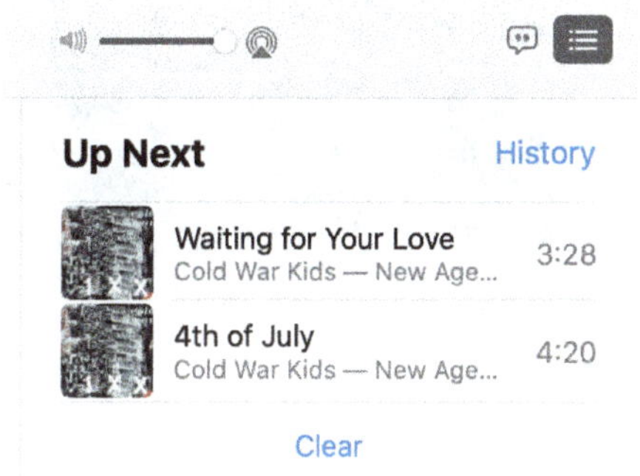

If you want to add a song to a playlist, then right-click the song and select the playlist (or create one).

At any point, you can tap the artist's name to see all of their music.

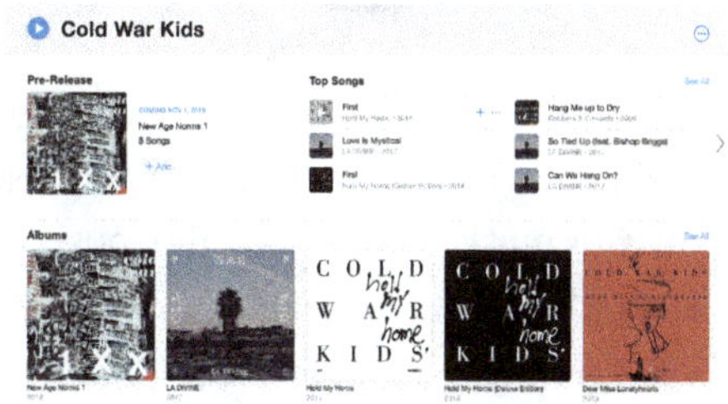

In addition to seeing information about the band, their popular songs, and their albums, you can get a playlist of their essential songs or a playlist of bands that they have influenced.

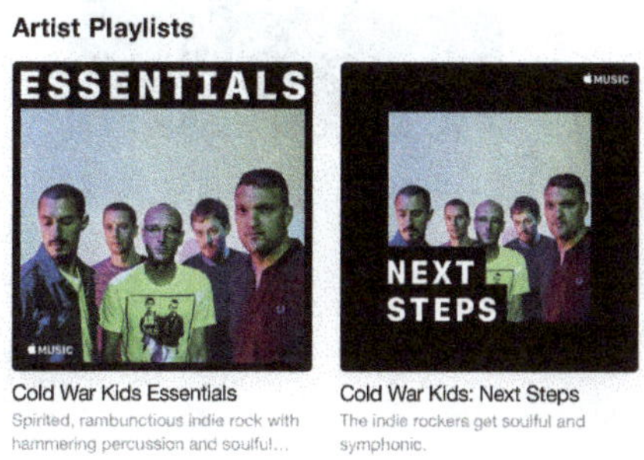

If you scroll to the bottom, you can also see Similar Artists, which is a great way to discover new bands that are like the ones you are currently listening to.

Tips for Getting the Most Out of Apple Music

Heart It

Like what you're hearing? Heart it! Hate it? Dislike it. Apple gets to know you by what you listen to, but it improves the accuracy when you tell it what you think of a song you are really into…or really hate.

Download Music

If you don't want to rely on wi-fi when you are on the go, make sure and tap the cloud on your music to download the music locally to your phone. If you don't see a cloud, add it to your library by tapping the plus, which should change it to a cloud.

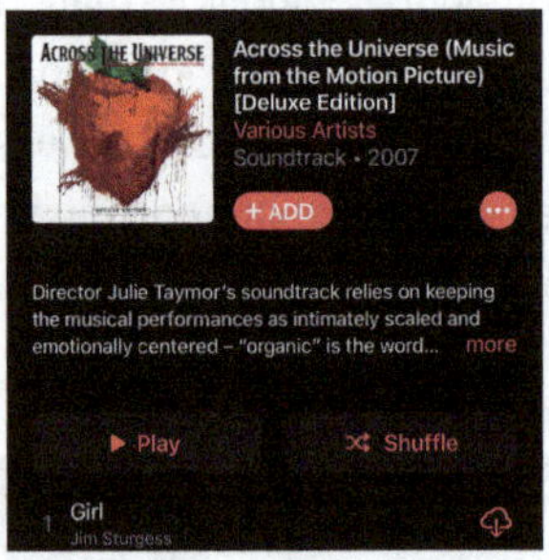

Hey Siri

Siri knows music! Say "Hey Siri" and say what you want to listen to, and the AI will get to work.

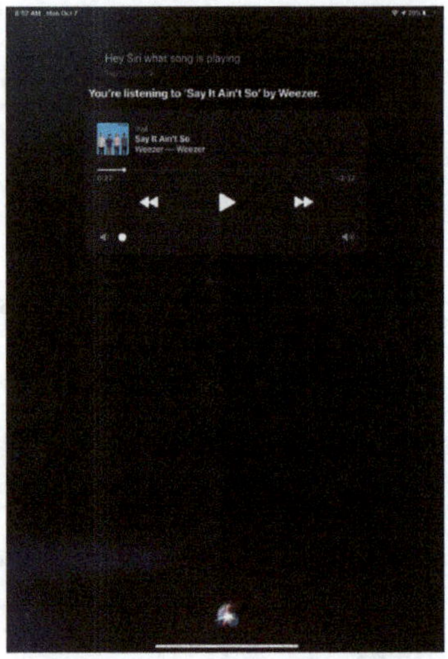

CHAPTER 9: HOW TO CUSTOMIZE THINGS

So now you know the basics; you should be able to work your way around the desktop with ease and use all the basic programs comfortably. But it still doesn't feel quite… you. It still has all the default settings, colors, gestures, and backgrounds. Sure it's a cool computer, but now let's make it feel like your computer.

System Preferences

All of the main settings are accessed in System Preferences which is essentially the Mac equivalent of Control Panel on a Windows computer. So to get started, let's get to System Preferences by clicking Launchpad, then clicking the System Preferences icon.

You can also get there by clicking on the Apple in the upper left corner of the menu and clicking System Preferences.

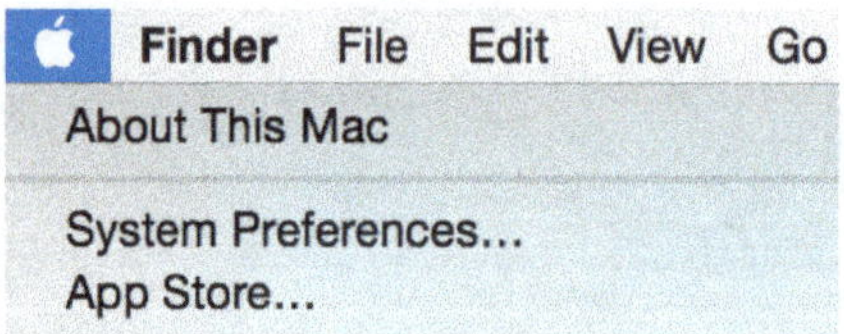

Once the app opens, you'll see there are lots of things that you can configure.

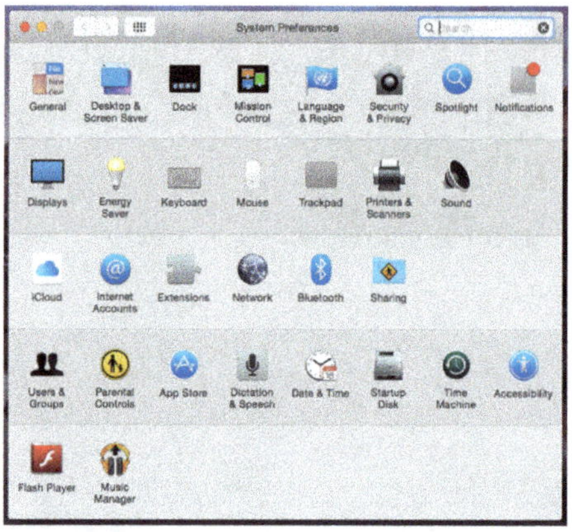

General

Let's get started with the first option: General. Under General, you can:

- Change the appearance of the main buttons, windows, and menus by selecting either Blue or Graphite.
- Choose the highlight color.
- Change the top menu bar and Dock to dark colors. This option works well with dark wallpapers.
- Set scroll bars to display automatically based on mouse or Trackpad, only when scrolling, or always on.
- Select the default web browser.

Here is where you can allow Handoff to work between your Mac and iCloud devices (some older Macs don't support this feature).

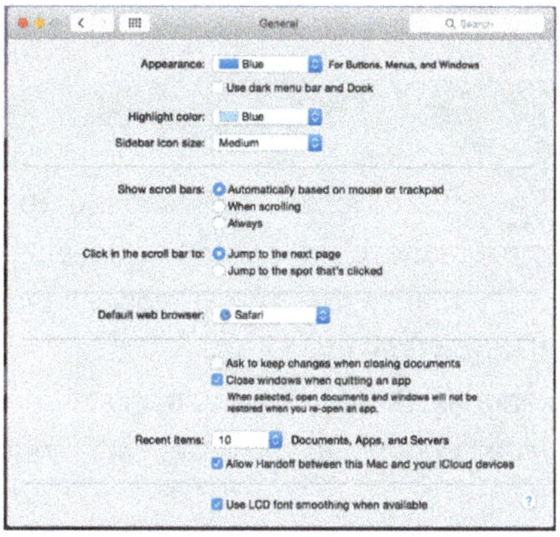

At any time, you can get back to the main System Preferences page by clicking on the button with 12 tiny squares. You can also hit the Back button, but if you are several menus in, you may have to hit the Back button several times.

Desktop & Screen Saver

The Desktop & Screen Saver section will help you change perhaps the most visually noticeable thing on your Mac—the desktop wallpaper. Along the left sidebar you will see several different dropdown options: Apple, iPhoto, and Folders.

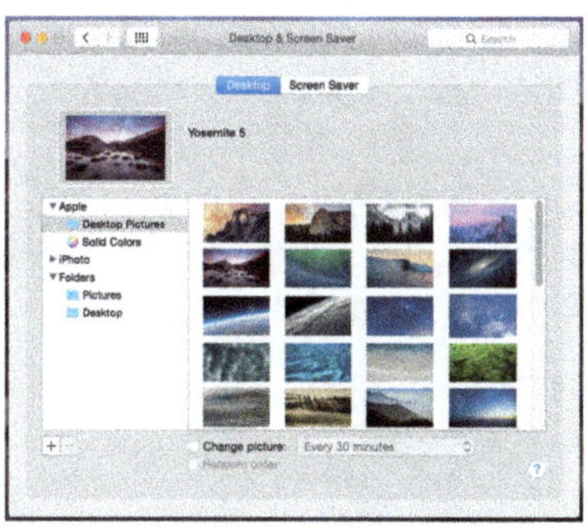

At the bottom, you will be able to change the picture every so often, and you can choose how often you'd like a new image to refresh. The images that show up in the right-hand window will be the ones that get scrolled through during refreshes.

To change your desktop wallpaper to one of the great-looking images provided by Apple, or if you just want to browse the available choices, click on the Apple name. A bunch of colorful, high-resolution images will populate the right-hand side, and you can scroll through the list to find something you like. Clicking on an image will change your wallpaper to that particular selection. If you're a plain Jane and prefer to keep things really simple, you can also select Solid Colors to find an array of potentially yawn-inducing plain wallpapers.

Selecting iPhoto will let you scroll through your photos, allowing you to select a cherished memory as your wallpaper.

The Folders option will let you choose between added folders where more image files might be lying in wait. If you save lots of images to your desktop, you might want to add the Desktop folder here so you can include those images as would-be wallpapers.

Adding and Removing Folders

To add new folders and image collections, click on the '+' button located at the bottom of the left sidebar.

When the window comes up, search for the folder that you'd like to add.

Once you find the desired folder, click the blue Choose button to confirm the changes.

To remove a folder, highlight the folder that you'd like deleted and then click the '–' button to remove it.

Screen Saver

To set one up, click on the Screen Saver button at the top of the Desktop & Screen Saver window.

The left sidebar will have more options than you probably need when it comes to different ways to display your pictures. Some great ones you will probably like are Shuffling Tiles, Vintage Prints, and Classic.

On the right side you can see a preview of what your screen saver will look like. In this part of the window you can also select a source: National Geographic, Aerial, Cosmos, Nature Patterns, and Choose Folder if you have a particular folder of images you'd like to use. If you'd like to shuffle the order in which images appear, check the box next to Shuffle slide order.

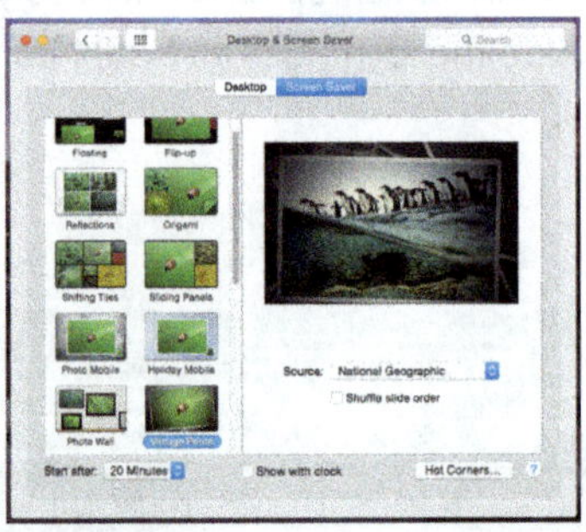

At the very bottom of the window you can choose the length of time before the screen saver starts. You'll also be able to pick if you'd like to display the clock or not.

Dock

There isn't a lot you can do to the Dock and most of these settings are self-explanatory. For the most part the settings just make things a little more…animated. Magnification, for example, makes an app icon larger when you hover your mouse over it.

One option I will point out, however, is the option to automatically hide and show Dock; all of these settings are a matter of taste; I personally choose to hide the Dock for two reasons: one, it gives you more screen space, and two, it lets you use the Dock while you are in a full screen app.

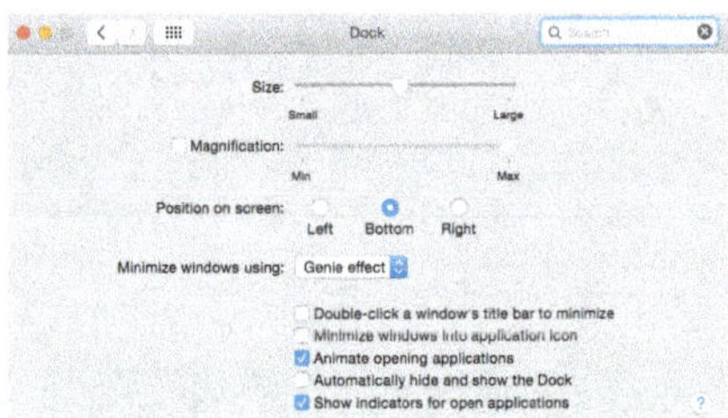

Mission Control

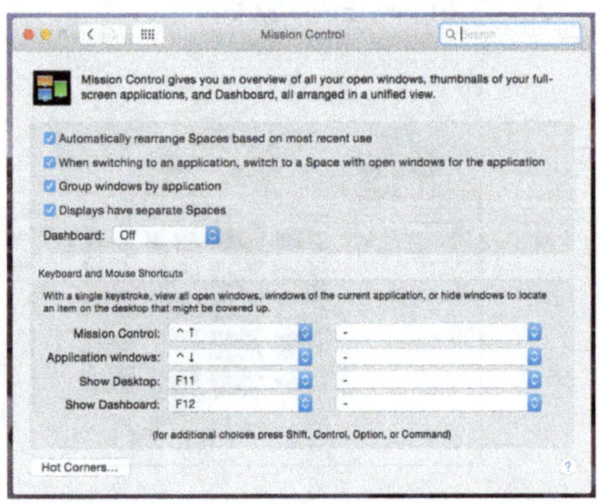

Mission Control is where you can set different parts of your screen to do different things. What do I mean by that? For example, you can set up a shortcut so that every time you move your mouse to the far upper right corner, your desktop is revealed. You can also set up shortcut keys on your keyboard. Mission Control is really about helping you make simple tasks quick.

Social Networking, Mail, Contacts and Calendars

When you use Twitter, Facebook and other apps, you may be used to just going to a website. On a Mac, you can add them into your computer's information, so you don't need to login; this also lets you get notification pop ups when you have new messages, likes, etc.

Adding Accounts

To add accounts, go to System Preferences on your Dock (the gears icon) and select Internet Accounts. From here, you can add accounts that haven't already been migrated, including iCloud, Exchange, Google, Twitter, Facebook, LinkedIn, Yahoo!, AOL, Vimeo and Flickr. Adding accounts here will start populating Catalina's native Mail, Contacts, Reminders and Calendar apps, and add options to your Share button.

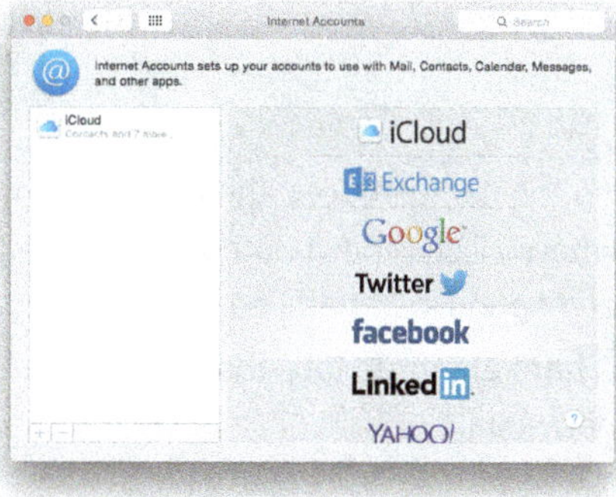

Note: You can also add accounts within the Mail, Contacts, Calendars, and Reminders apps by opening each app and clicking File > Add Account.

Twitter, Facebook, LinkedIn, Vimeo and Flickr

Catalina OS supports deep Twitter, Facebook, LinkedIn, Flickr and Vimeo integration. To get started, simply sign in to your account(s) from System Preferences > Internet Accounts. Select Twitter, Facebook, LinkedIn, Flickr, or Vimeo, and then enter your username and password. From now on, you'll be able to use that account with the Share button throughout Catalina and receive notifications in your Notifications Center.

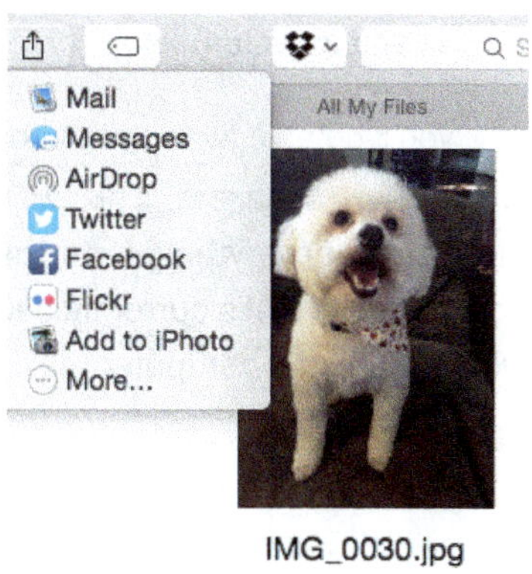

Sound

As the name implies, the Sound menu is where all changes related to sound effects and sound in general can be modified.

There are three tabs that you can switch between.

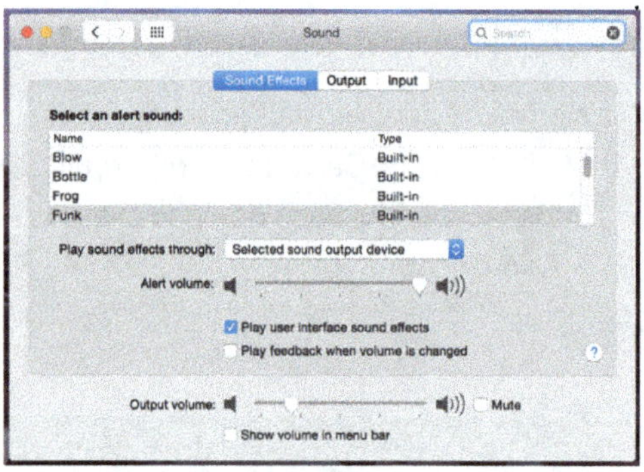

Sound Effects

The Sound Effects tab is where you can select an alert sound from the many different built-in options. By default, the following dropdown menu should be set to Selected sound output device to play the chosen sound effects through your standard speakers.

The next two checkboxes let you turn sound effects on or off for the user interface, and for volume control.

Lastly, you'll be able to adjust the output volume of your speakers. This will affect the loudness of everything from sound effects to music that's currently being played through the computer.

Input & Output

The input and output tabs are both very similar. Each will let you change the device for sound input or output (speakers or microphones), as well as adjust sound settings. In the output tab, you can adjust the slider to move the balance left or right, and in input, you can change the microphone's input volume and enable or disable the built-in noise reduction feature in case you frequently use your Mac's microphone in busy cafes.

Users & Groups

If your Mac is for family use and a couple of people will be using it, then this setting will come in handy.

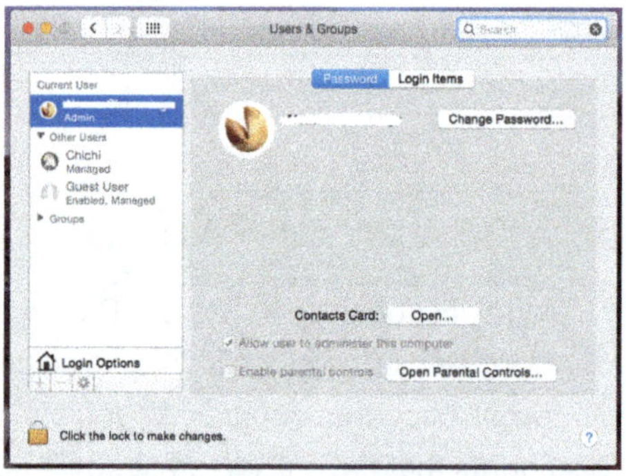

Along the left sidebar all existing users and groups (if you have any) will be laid out for you. To make a change to an existing user, first you need to choose the "Click the lock" icon and unlock it; unlocking lets you change settings to the user. You will also be asked for your password at this time—this is all a safety measure to ensure that if you accidentally left your computer unattended, someone couldn't come along and lock you out of your own machine.

Below are a few things you'll be able to do with each user. Depending on the type of user it is (admin, guest, child, etc.), some of the settings won't be available.

Selecting the admin user account will let you change the login password, open up the Contacts card and enable parental controls. Clicking the Login Items will allow you to change the applications that start running automatically each time you log in. There has to be at least one admin user.

Any other created users that you make will have options to enable parental controls, change password, or turn that account into another administrator account that has full control of the Mac.

By default, you will see a guest user set up. If it's selected, you can choose to disable the guest user from being available as a login option. You can also set parental controls and allow guest access to your shared folders. If you do choose to keep the guest user, keep in mind that there will be no password required, and all information and files created during that session will be deleted upon logging out.

At the bottom of the left sidebar there is another option, called Login Options. This is where you'll find different options such as automatic login, show password hints, and show the Sleep, Shut Down, and Restart buttons. You can also display your full name or user name at the top right of the menu bar by checking the box next to Show fast user switching menu and making a selection.

Create New Users

So you know how to manage the primary user, but what about creating additional users? That's pretty simple. Just follow these steps (and make sure you have already hit that lock button to unlock the option).

Click on the '+' button.

From the New Account dropdown menu, choose from the following options: Administrator, Standard, Managed with Parental Controls, or Sharing Only.

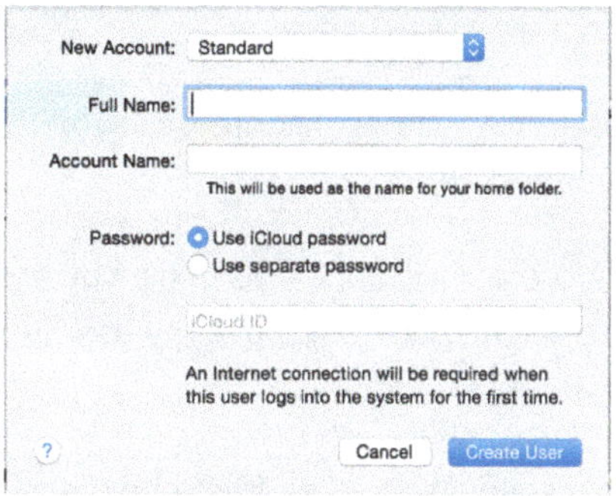

Fill in the Full Name and Account Name fields. These don't have to be real names. Mickey Mouse can have a user name if you want.

You can choose to have the new user log in using an existing iCloud account and password, or create a whole new password.

If you selected Use iCloud Password, you will be prompted to enter the associated iCloud ID.

If you instead choose to opt for a newly-created password, you will be asked to enter it twice to verify it.

Once finished, click the blue Create User button. If you chose to use an iCloud ID, you will be asked to enter the password. If you made a new password, you don't need to do anything else.

Removing Existing Users

Just because you added a user, that doesn't mean they're there forever. You can delete them at any time. But remember, deleting them deletes all the settings they've set up —so if you create that user again, everything will be gone.

To remove current users, select the user that you'd like to delete.

With that user highlighted, click on the '– ' button.

A prompt will appear asking if you are really sure you'd like to remove the user from the computer.

You can also choose from one of three radio buttons: save the home folder, leave the home folder alone, or delete the home folder.

Once you've made a decision, click the blue Delete User button to confirm your choice and make the changes happen.

Creating Groups

If the computer is being used in a place where there are dozens of users (a classroom or library, perhaps), then creating a group would be a good option for you.

At the bottom of the left sidebar, click the '+' button.

From the New dropdown menu, select Group

In the Full Name field, create and enter a name for your group.

Click the blue Create Group button to confirm.

The new group will be created, and you will be able to check boxes next to each existing user to designate who will be a part of this group. If you have existing groups, you can also select entire groups to be a part of yet another group.

Snap This

Screenshots on MacOS have always been pretty simple and straightforward. Shift-Command-3 to take a screenshot of your entire screen and Shift-Command-4 to take a screenshot of a specific area of your screen.

These commands still work, but Apple took it up a notch and allows you to edit the screenshot—if you've taken screenshots on iOS, then the experience is probably familiar to you.

As soon as you take a screenshot, you'll see options for what you can do next in a small popup at the bottom right of your screen. These options will take you to a Markup window where you can add annotations, shapes, text, and more.

In addition to these options, MacOS has added a new command: Shift-Command-5. This opens up a screenshot interface with several options such as capture entire screen, selected window, or a selected portion. The last two options are new:

record the entire screen or record a portion of it.

Continue That Photo Where You Left Off

One thing Apple has done really well with their devices is continuity—the idea of stopping on one device and picking up where you left off on another. For example, you could stop a movie in the living room on Apple TV and continue watching it on your Apple TV in the bedroom. Or you could get a text on your Apple Watch and reply on your phone. It's all very intuitive and just works.

This concept of using on one device and picking up on another now extends to the camera. With OS Catalina, you can take a picture on your iPhone or iPad and have it automatically sent to your Mac and into the photo editing app of your desire.

If the Mac app supports the feature, then you'll see it under Edit in the menu area; there will be a new option that says "Insert from Your iPhone or iPad" with the option to Take Photo or Scan Documents.

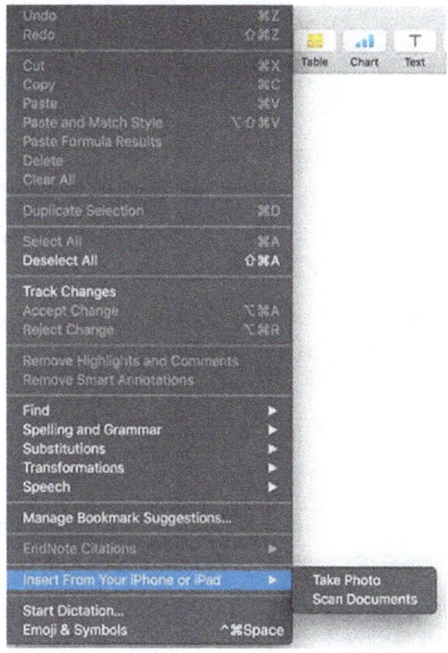

Once you snap the photo on your phone or tablet, it will automatically appear in the document.

Accessibility

Accessibility helps you adjust the computer if you have any kind of impairment or disability. It lets you change things like making the display larger, having a voiceover that describes what's on your screen, and put captions on videos when available.

To open Accessibility, click System Settings and Accessibility. On the left side of the box that comes up will be all the various things you can change. Clicking on each one will create more options.

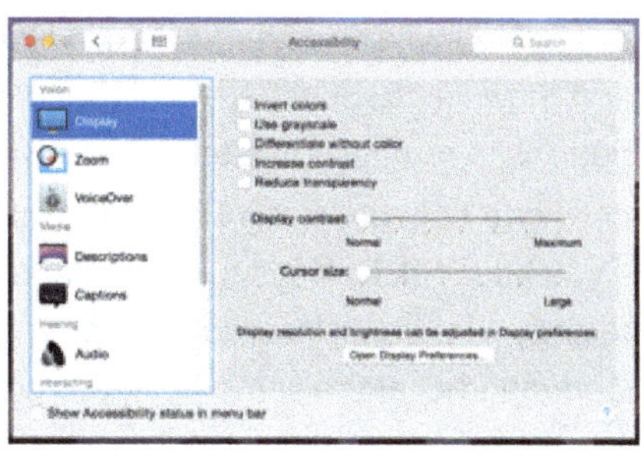

Vision

Under Display, you can make the screen grayscale, invert colors, decrease the contrast, etc. Zoom allows you to create a zoom effect over smaller areas of the screen when you hit a keyboard shortcut. VoiceOver reads back any text that's on the screen.

Media

The Media section includes a few different settings for audio and video playback. Click on Descriptions to enable spoken descriptions for videos.

Captions will apply subtitles and captions to videos.

Hearing

The Sound tab provides options for the hearing disabled. You can choose to set up a visual flash of the screen each time an alert sound is played, and also decide if you'd like to play stereo audio as mono instead.

Interacting

Keyboard includes settings for Sticky Keys and Slow Keys. Sticky Keys allows certain buttons to remain activated without you having to hold down the key. For example, if you have Sticky Keys turned on and want to copy some text, instead of holding down Command-C at the same time, you could press the Command button first, followed by the C key. When enabled, you'll hear a lock sound, and any time you use a modifier key like Command, a large icon will appear in the top right corner of the screen indicating that a Sticky Key combination has been started. Slow Keys increases the amount of time between a button press and activation, so if you press Enter, it will take a little longer to actually process.

Mouse & Trackpad features settings like Mouse Keys, which lets you move the mouse around using the number pad on your keyboard, double-click speed, and the option to ignore the built-in Trackpad (on MacBooks) if there is a separate mouse or Trackpad connected to the computer.

Switch Control requires you to enter your administrator password before making any changes, because it's a powerful function that allows you to control the computer using one or more switches that you designate. You can also modify other settings like what to do while navigating, determine pointer precision, and change the size for the Switch Control cursor.

The Dictation tab does exactly what it sounds like—it lets you dictate commands and write or edit text using only your voice. To enable dictation, you first need to click on the bottom button that says Open Dictation & Speech Preferences and selecting the On radio button.

Voice Control

Voice Control lets you control your computer with your voice.

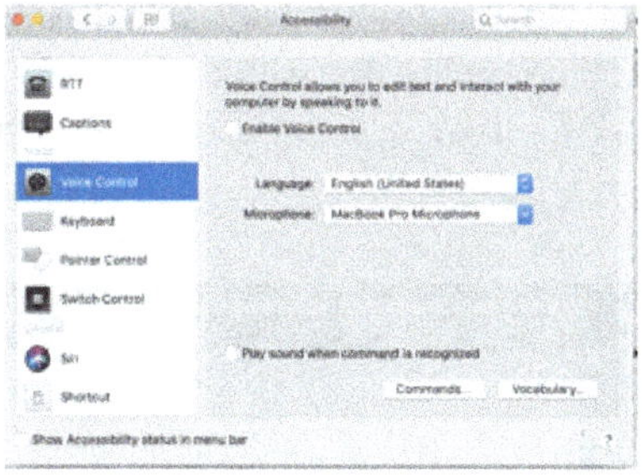

SIDECAR

What's Sidecar? It's basically using your iPad as a second screen alongside your Mac.

Using your iPad as a second Mac screen is nothing new. Popular apps such as Duet have been doing this successfully for years.

Apple has finally taken note and decided to release a feature called Sidecar that lets you wirelessly use your iPad as a secondary Mac screen; it's just like using AirPlay on your phone to show YouTube on your TV. So long apps like Duet, right? Not exactly.

Before moving into how to use Sidecar, let me first mention what Sidecar is not: a rich app full of pro features. It does one thing very well: shows your Mac screen on your iPad. Apps like Duet are compatible with iPhone and iPad and also work with cross OSes—so you can also show your Windows device on your iPad. But personally, one thing I find lacking on Sidecar is touch. I expected to be able to tap the iPad screen and launch apps and folders. That wasn't the case. It was for display purposes only...unless you have an Apple Pencil. Sidecar feels like it was made to entice people to buy an Apple Pencil. With an Apple Pencil, touch suddenly becomes possible. There's probably a good reason for this—the Apple Pencil is more precise and has more gestures than your finger.

So now that you know a little about what it isn't, let's look at how it works.

First, make sure your MacBook (yes, this is only compatible with MacBooks—sorry Windows users) is up-to-date with the latest OS (Catalina).

Second, make sure your iPad is turned on, in standby mode, and on the same Wi-Fi network (if not, you won't see the next step).

Third, go to the menu in the upper right side of your MacBook and click the rectangular box for AirPlay.

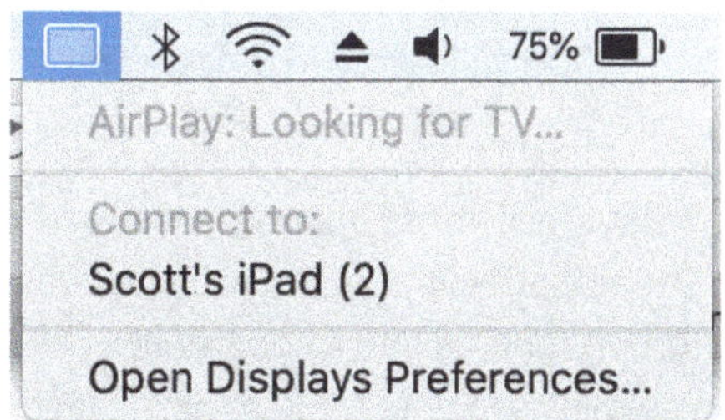

That's it! Kind of. Your MacBook should now be showing on your iPad. It will look a little like this:

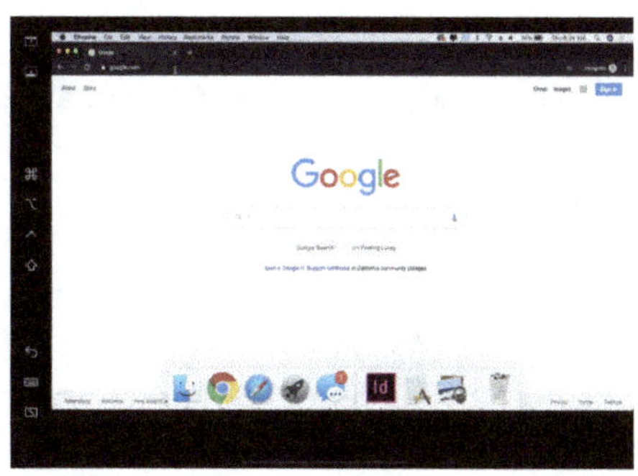

So what do I mean "kind of"? There are still a few more settings you should know about.

Click that AirPlay box in the right corner again and you'll see even more options.

What are all these options? Use As Separate Display (vs the two Mirror options) turns your iPad into a second screen—so you can have another Mac app running on your display instead of just showing whatever is on your MacBook. The two Hide options get rid of the boxes you see on your iPad to make it a bit more full screen.

Finally, Open Sidecar Preferences will give you a few additional options. You can, for example, pick to show the menu bar on the right instead of left.

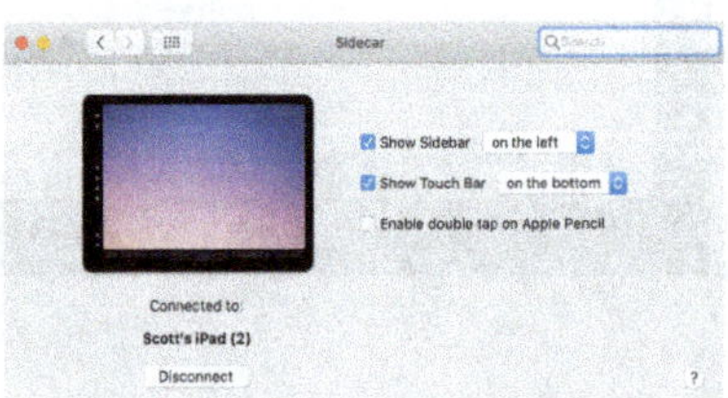

You can disconnect from Sidecar by either tapping on the box with the line through it on your iPad or going to the AirPlay button on your Mac and disconnecting.

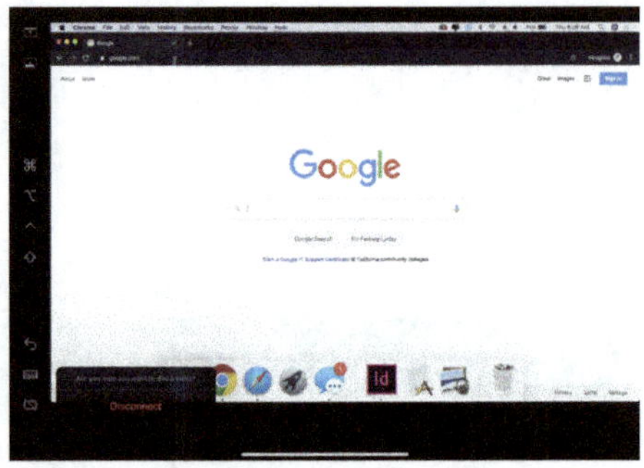

Security

If your computer is in a place where other people can get to it, or if you are just generally concerned about your privacy being violated, then head on over to Privacy and Security in the System Preferences.

Creating Strong Passwords

Strong passwords are the first line of defense against potential hackers (or smart children!); a strong password is not something like "password"; a strong password has letters, numbers and even symbols in it. It could be something like this: "@mY_MACb00k."

You can use the Password Assistant to test how strong your password is.

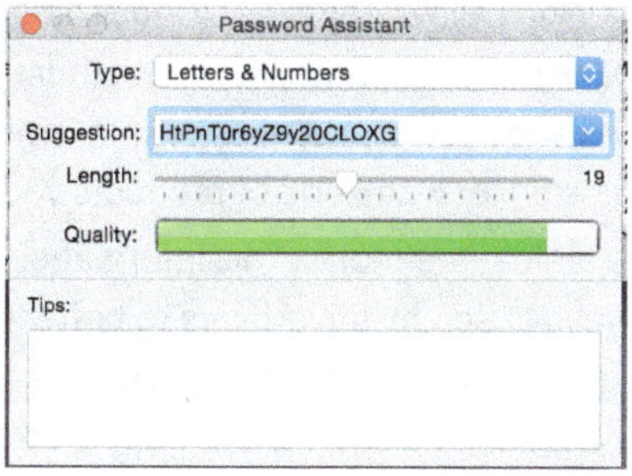

When Keychain loads, you will be able to view the entire list of accounts that are already synced to Keychain. If you would like to change the password for an account that already exists, find the account and double-click on it. If not, click on the '+' button at the bottom to add a new account.

When the new window comes up, take a look at the bottom. There will be a field for password, and at the right of it will be a small key icon. Click the key icon to open up Password Assistant.

From Type you can select Manual (create your own), Memorable, Letters & Numbers, Numbers Only, Random, and FIPS-181 compliant.

Suggestions will automatically populate, and you can scroll through several different suggestions by using the dropdown menu.

Adjust the length slider to make the password longer or shorter. Any password you create will meet at least these requirements to be considered fair.

As you generate a password, the quality indicator will change to show you how safe and complex a given password is.

Firewall

Another line of defense you can add is a firewall, which protects you from unwanted connections to potentially malicious software applications, websites, or files.

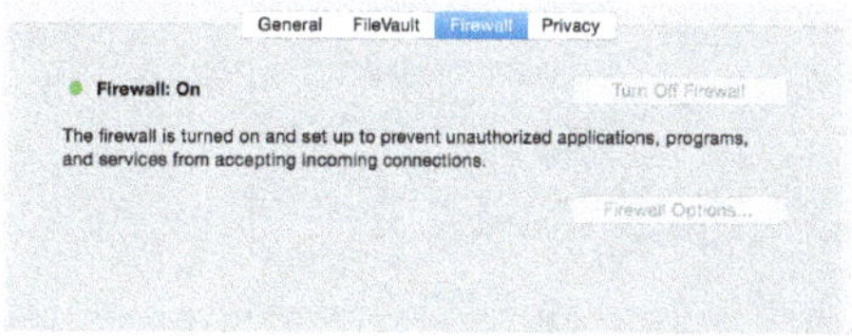

To enable the firewall that comes with your Mac, go to System Preferences > Security & Privacy and select the Firewall tab.

Before you can make any changes, click on the lock icon in the bottom left corner and enter your administrator password to continue.

Find My Mac

Just like your iPhone or iPad, Mac comes with a handy feature called "Find My Mac" which lets you find your computer if someone steals it or you just misplace it; you can also wipe its hard drive clean remotely.

To enable Find My Mac, go to System Preferences > iCloud and check the box next to Find My Mac. Your location services must also be turned on, so go to System Preferences > Security & Privacy > Privacy > Location Services and make sure Enable Location Services is checked on.

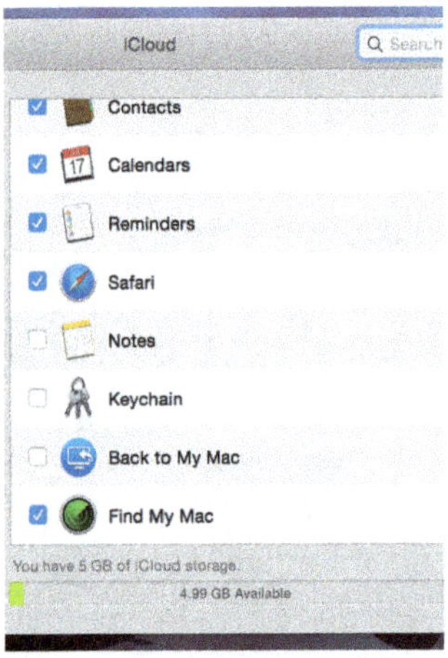

To track your computer, you can log into any computer and visit iCloud.com, enter your iCloud login information, and click on Find My Mac. As long as the Mac is awake and connected to the Internet through Wi-Fi or Ethernet, you will be able to play a loud sound, lock it, or completely erase it so your private information is removed.

Privacy

Apple knows people worry about privacy; they have lots built in to help you control what can (and can't) be seen.

Internet Privacy

If you'd like to clear your search and browsing history, there are two ways to do it: either by clicking on Safari > Clear History and Website Data or History > Clear History and Website Data. Both can be found on the top menu bar. When the window comes up, you will be able to choose how far back you want the clearing to reach. Once you make a selection just press the Clear History button to make the changes final.

Cookies allow websites to store data and track certain things, like what other websites you visit during your Internet session, or what kind of products you tend to look at the most. This information is mostly used by advertisers to better target ads for you, but the option is always there if you'd like to disable them. Open up Safari, go to Safari > Preferences, then select the Privacy tab. The cookie options range from allowing all websites to store cookies to blocking all websites. You can also allow cookies only from the most frequently visited websites. If you prefer not to be tracked, check off the box at the bottom that says Ask Websites To Not Track Me. Some websites will not function as you may want them to by disabling this feature.

Application Privacy

The other part of privacy is through installed applications. Go to System Preferences > Security & Privacy and click the Privacy tab. You can shut Location Services off by checking the box next to Enable Location Services. Browse through the left sidebar and you'll be able to customize permissions. If you don't want any apps to access your contacts or calendars, here is where you can block some or all programs from that information.

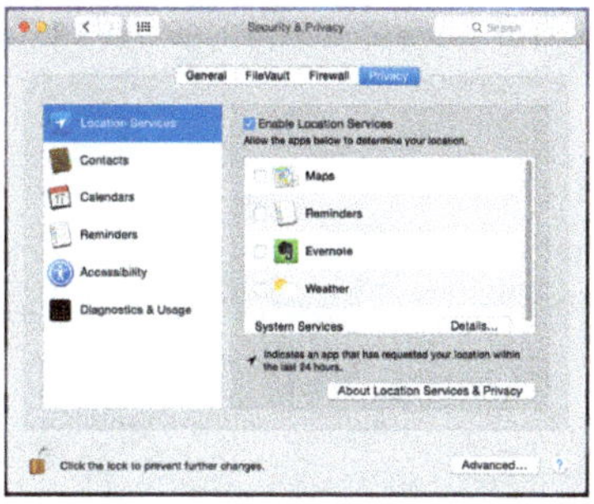

Screen Time

Screen Time might be something you are familiar with. It's been on iPads and iPhones for a while. It comes to MacOS with the Catalina update. What is it? It's a productivity setting that lets you restrict how long you can use certain apps (games for instance). It's highly customizable, so you can set one app like Word to have zero restrictions, but another one like Internet to have limits.

Screen Time isn't an app in the traditional sense; it's an app within your system settings. To use it, go to System Preferences, then click Screen Time.

This launches a new window that tells you how much time you've been on your computer.

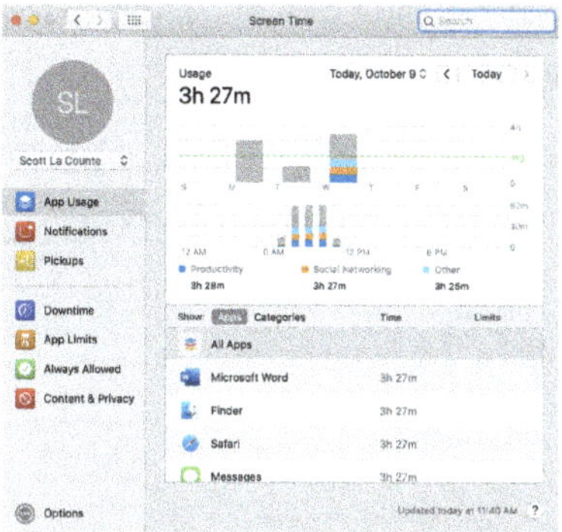

You can set up a passcode by clicking on options at the bottom of the window.

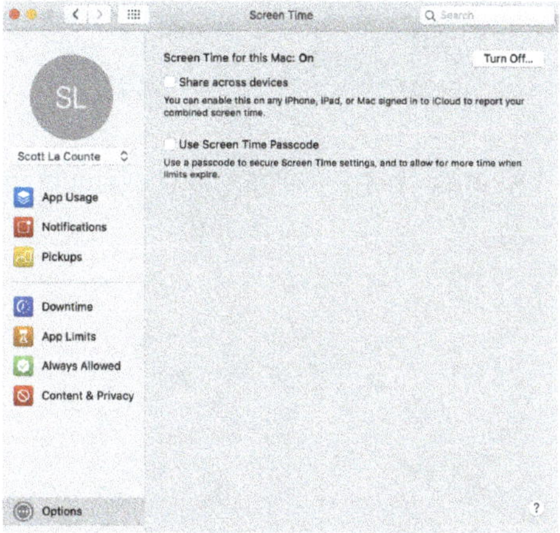

App Limits is where you can start restricting certain apps. Click the '+' in this section.

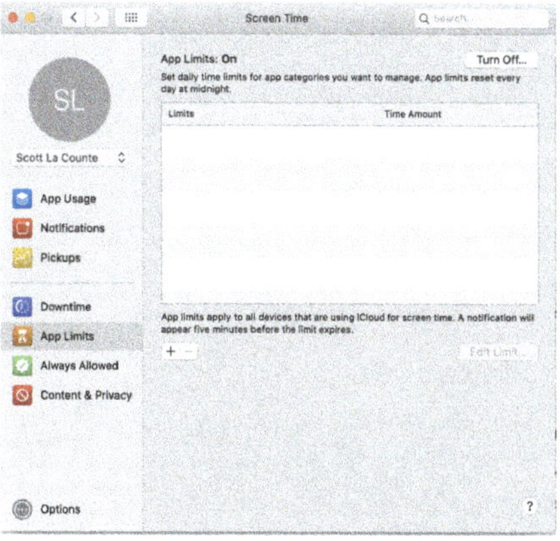

From here select the app (or kinds of apps) that you want to limit.

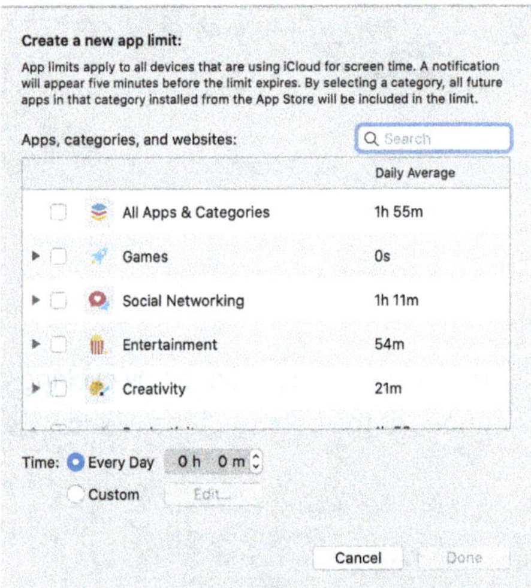

At the bottom, you can say how much time you want to set the limit to.

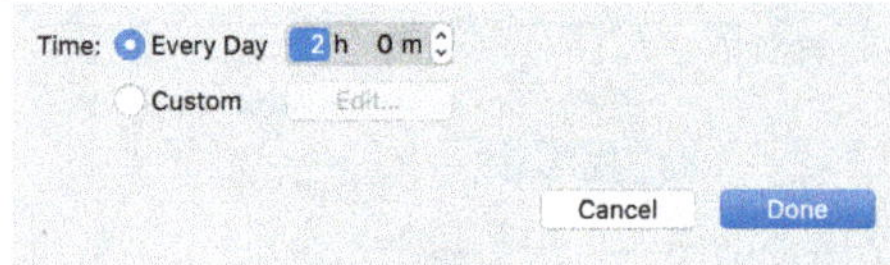

Under Always Allow, you can select apps that have no restrictions.

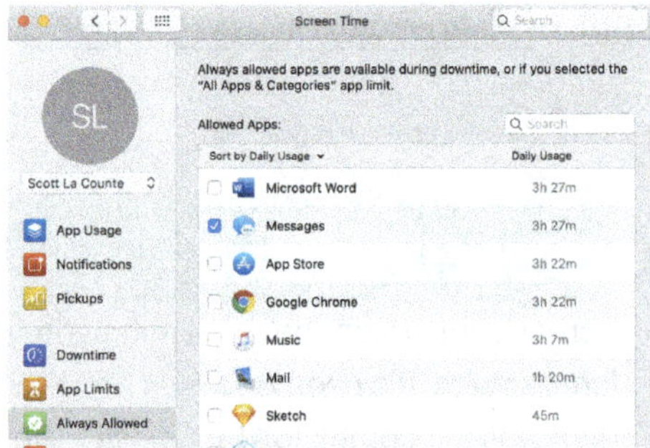

Chapter 10: Keep It running Smoothly

Macs feel more like an investment than other computers; with that in mind, you obviously want to protect and maintain your investment. In this chapter, I'll cover how.

Time Machine

Everyone worries about losing their data; Apple helps you out with one of their most powerful behind-the-scenes apps: Time Machine.

Time Machine will back up all of your files, applications, and settings with minimal configuration or headache. In the case of a catastrophic event such as hard drive failure, having a Time Machine backup can allow you to quickly recover all of your data and applications, and even all of your settings (such as your desktop background and even the specific location of icons on your desktop).

You will need to buy an external USB or Thunderbolt hard drive. It is recommended to buy a drive that is larger than the current used space on your computer. For example, if you have used 100 gigabytes of space on your computer's hard drive, you should buy at least a 120-gigabyte hard drive.

You can also purchase an additional Time Machine Airport Capsule that does all of this wirelessly.

To get started, plug the hard drive into your computer and Time Machine will start automatically. It will ask you if you would like to use the drive as a Time Machine Backup Disk. Choose Use as Backup Disk.

If Time Machine does not start automatically, go to Finder > Applications > Machine, and click Choose Backup Disk. Select your new hard drive.

After you specify the drive to use as a backup, Time Machine will automatically begin backing up your data.

Software Updates

If you want your computer running smoothly then make sure you update regularly; updates are free and come once every couple of months. They fix minor bugs and sometimes add things to correct vulnerabilities that might make your computer open to viruses.

MacOS X, by default, will prompt you when updates are available, and you need only to click "Update" and enter your password in order to run the updates. Sometimes, in the case of major updates, you will need to restart your computer to complete the update. You can click Not now if you would like to delay the updates until a more convenient time.

Bonus Book: Using Gmail

INTRODUCTION

Remember back when communications meant picking up a phone? Some people still do that, but email has become the method of choice for most communications. And that's great! But if all you know how to do is compose and send, then you are missing out on a lot of important features.

While there are many platforms for email, Gmail is perhaps the most popular. Gmail is also one of the most featured packed! There's so much that you probably don't even know about.

This guide, **in full color**, will walk you through things like making sure Spam doesn't show up in your inbox, how to use labels, and how to forward to other inboxes.

If you want to be a power user, then read on!

Ready to get started? Let's go!

Chapter 1: Gmail Crash Course

I'm going to go quickly through this chapter. Don't worry! This is just a high-level overview. I'll slow down in future chapters to drill a little deeper into different subjects.

One thing to note: this book only covers the desktop version of Gmail; the mobile version is very much the same, but there are a few extra things—notably swipe gestures. Once you understand the desktop version, you should have no problem with the mobile app.

First things first: How do you get an email? If you already have one, great! Skip this part! In fact, you might find yourself skipping around a lot. This book is for beginning and more experienced users alike, so if you've already been using Gmail for a while, then you may jump ahead.

As a side note, you can have as many email addresses as you like—personally, I have a family one, a business one, and a bogus one (which I use to fill out forms for companies I'm not sure if I trust). So if you already have one, feel free to create another!

To get started, go to gmail.com. You'll be greeted by a very simple webpage. It's asking you to sign in. How do you sign in when you don't have an account? You don't, obviously! Just click the Create account button under the sign-in box to get started. (Note: Anytime you need to access email after you have created an email, start at this page):

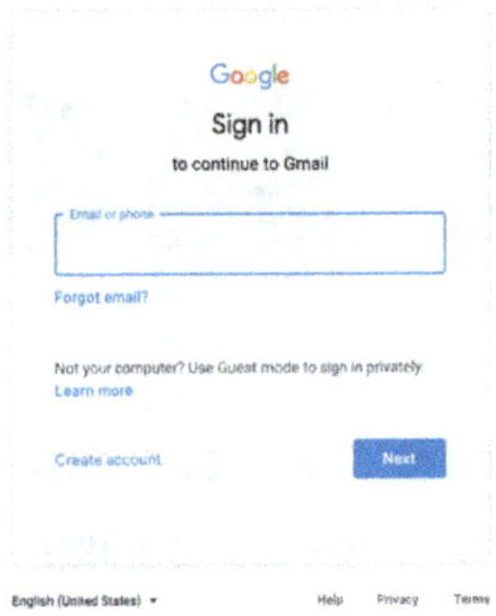

When you select Create account, it's going to ask if it's for yourself or a business:

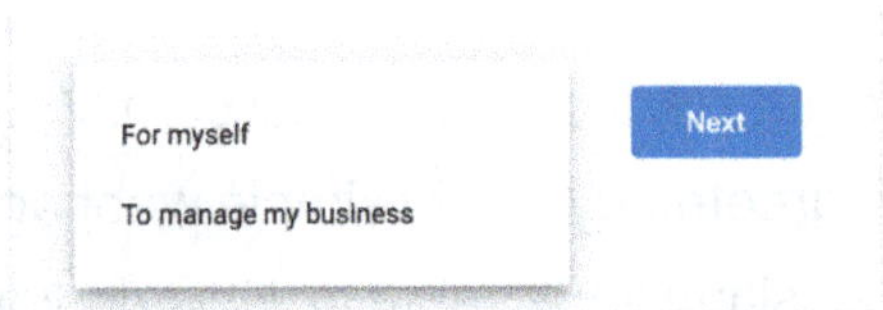

If you select business, Google's going to sell you on having a business account. That lets you use Gmail, but have your company's @ extension. Many businesses use the free personal version for their business—especially when they're just getting started.

Next, fill out the Google Account info, and hit Next:

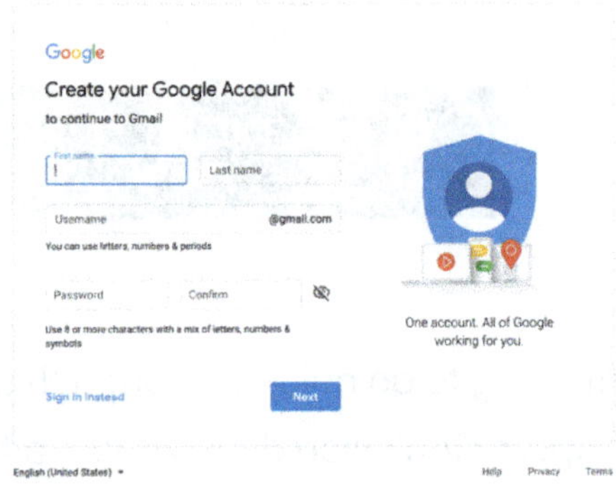

Remember I said an account could be bogus? Here I am creating one for Jonah Simms (in case you don't know, that's the name of a fictional character on the NBC show Superstore):

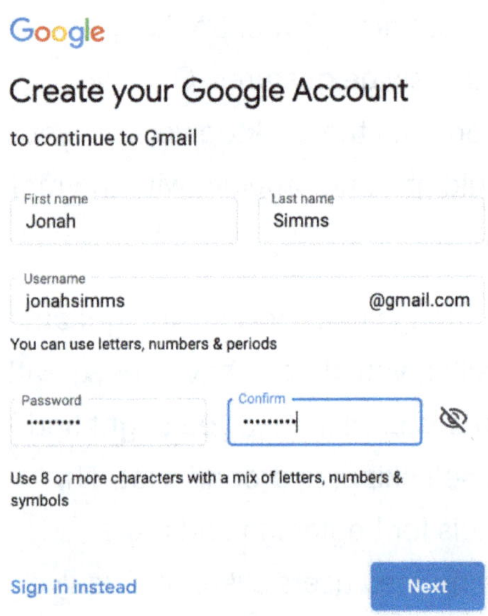

Turns out I'm not the only person who is a fan of Jonah Simms—my guess is there actually is a Jonah Simms in the world. In any case, my first choice for email is gone:

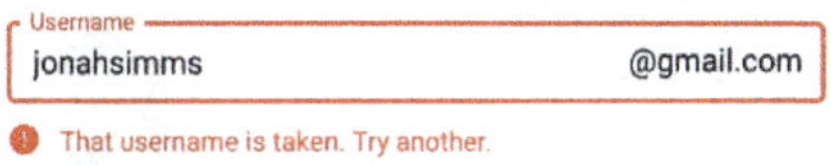

You might get the same error message—with over a billion Gmail accounts out there, many usernames are taken. Just keep thinking of new ones until you find one that's not taken. I just added a number 2 to mine.

Next, Gmail will ask some more personal information about you:

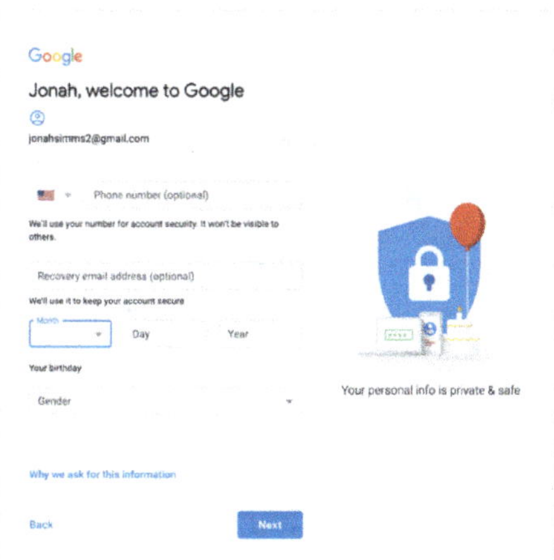

Why do they want to know this? If you really want to know, click the hyperlink, and it will tell you:

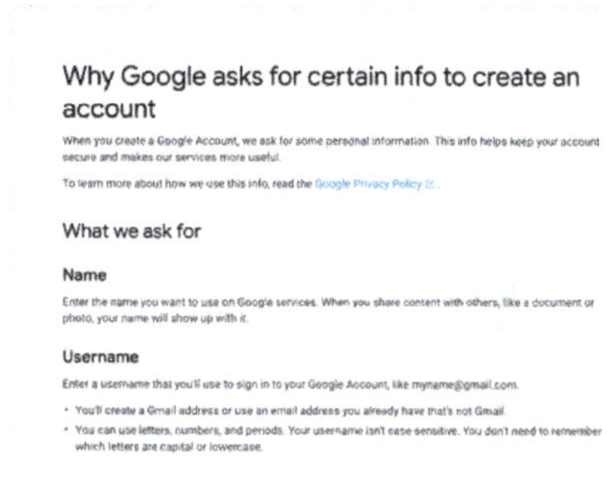

Most the fields are optional. Even the gender field has an option for not saying—and one for creating a custom gender:

Privacy is big with Google. The next page has a very lengthy Terms of Service. Is creating a bogus account in violation of these terms? Feel free to read this lengthy legal document to find out!

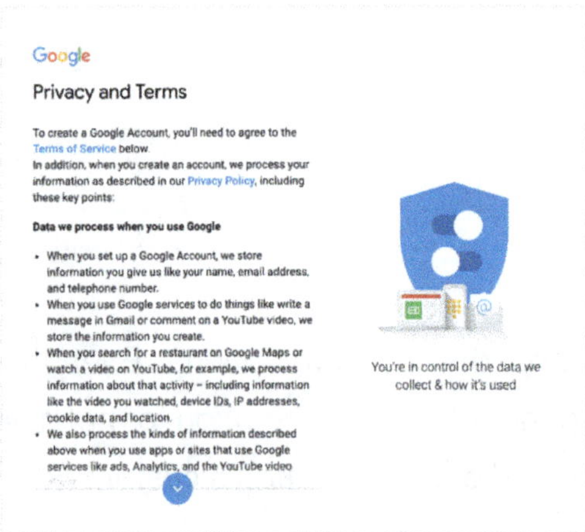

Or be like everyone else and scroll until the end and hit I agree:

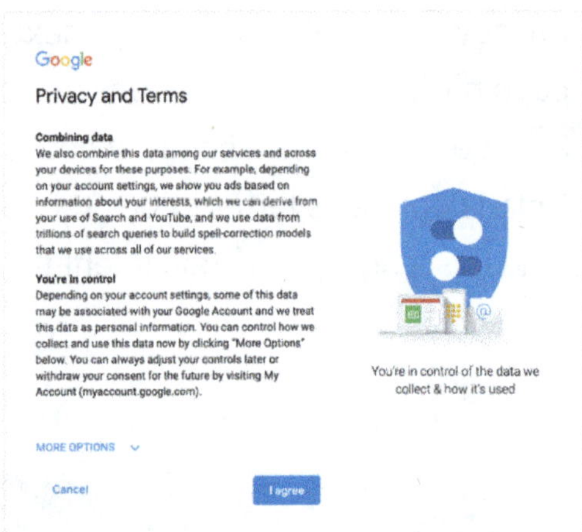

Congrats! You now have email!

When you hit Next, Gmail will ask what kind of view you want. There are three. The first is the default view that most people select:

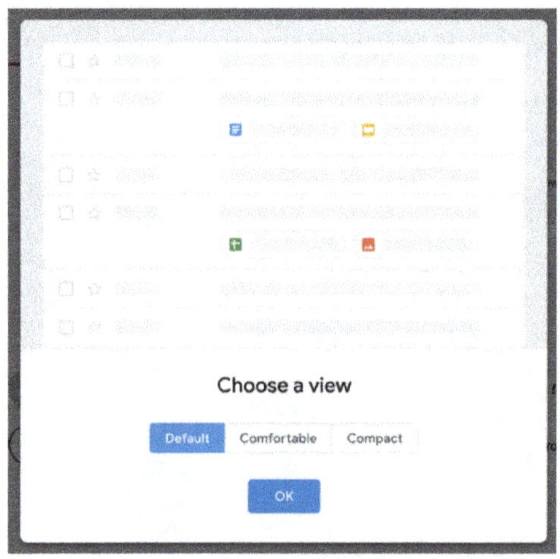

It's simple and it shows attachments—by that, I mean you can open attachments without opening the email.

Next is Comfortable; it's a little simpler. That open attachment option is gone and you'll see instead a paperclip next to emails with attachments:

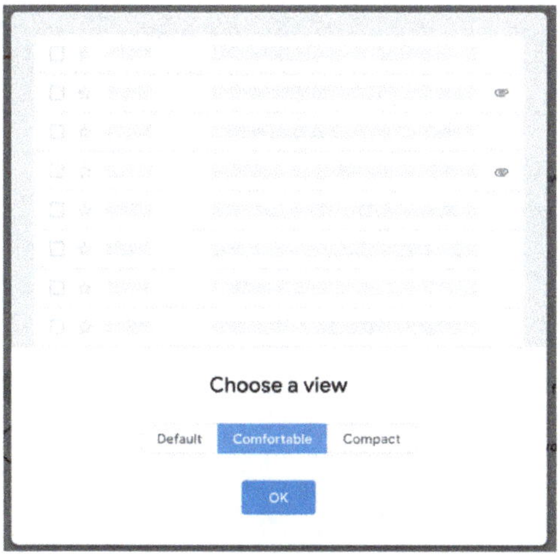

The last option is Compact. This is very similar to the Comfortable theme, but it's more compressed so you can see more emails on your screen. None work better than the other—it's just a preference (one that can be changed). When you have picked the one you want, select OK:

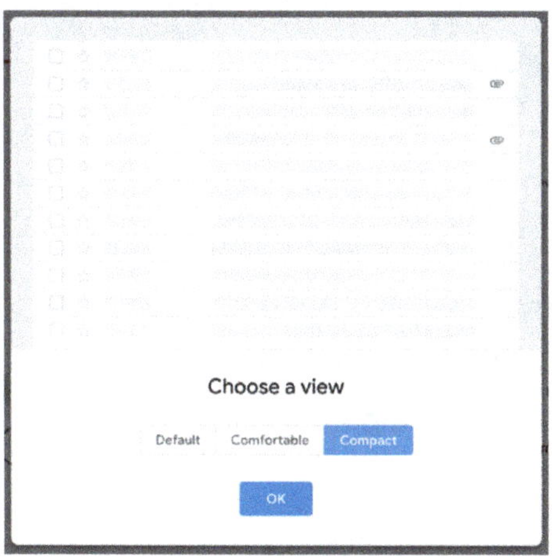

You'll now have access to all of your email—it's going to be empty right now, obviously:

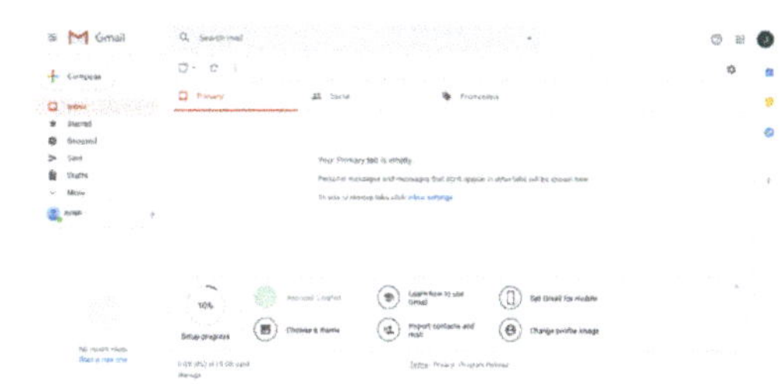

The menu on the left side is the one you'll use the most. Very quickly (again, we'll cover this more later), you'll see your main Inbox, Starred mail (this means you've basically flagged email to go in a special area), Snoozed (email that will return to your email at a later date), Sent, Drafts (if you accidently close an email before its sent, it will go here), and finally, More:

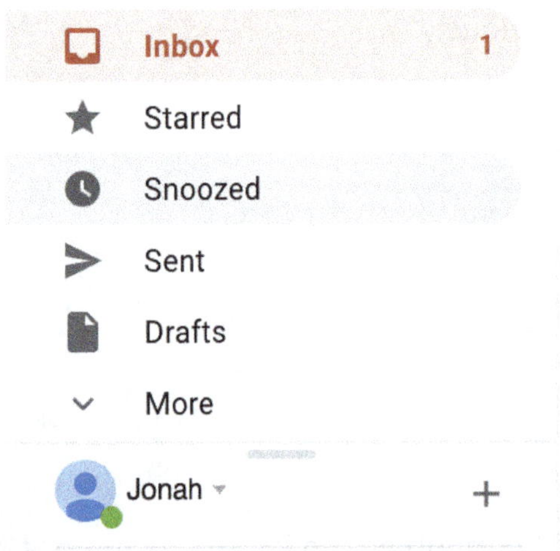

Selecting More brings up a larger menu. The thing you'll use the most here is probably Spam and Trash (where deleted emails go). Why would you use Spam? It's not uncommon for important emails to go here. It's a good idea to check it every day or every other day. If you aren't entering contests 24/7, then you shouldn't get a lot of Spam:

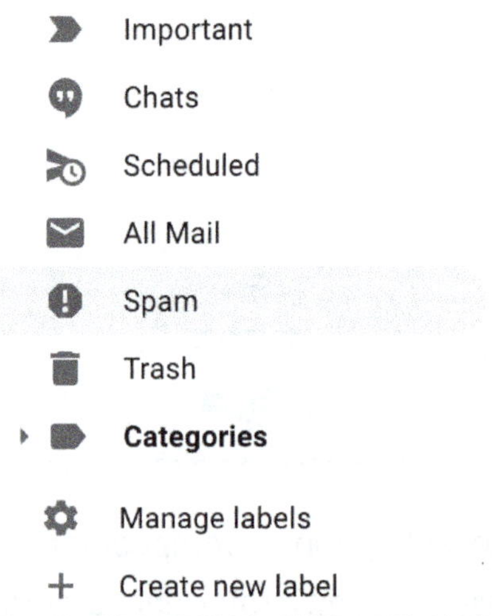

Above this menu is the Compose button; you'll click that to start a new email:

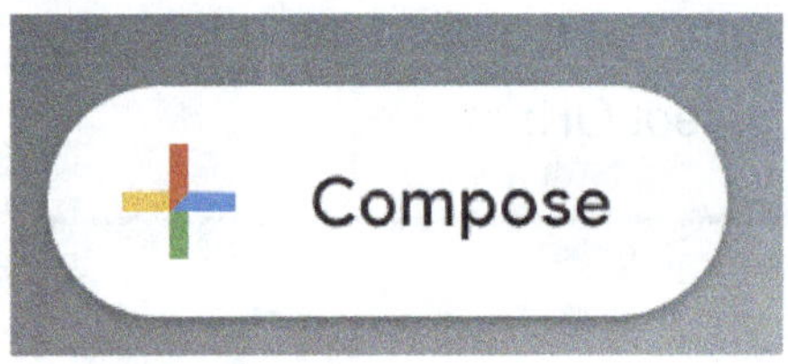

Next to Compose is a button with three lines. That expands and collapses your menu. Click it once and watch it collapse and become more narrow. Click it again and it goes back to normal:

Below the menu is a dialog box with a quotation. That's where you go to start a Hangout (a Hangout is like a video call—another free service from Google), or chat with someone:

To the right of Hangouts, you can see how much space you've used. Unless you send a lot of attachments, you'll probably never exceed it. If you do, you can buy more space very cheaply. As of this writing, you can get 100 GB for 20 bucks a year.

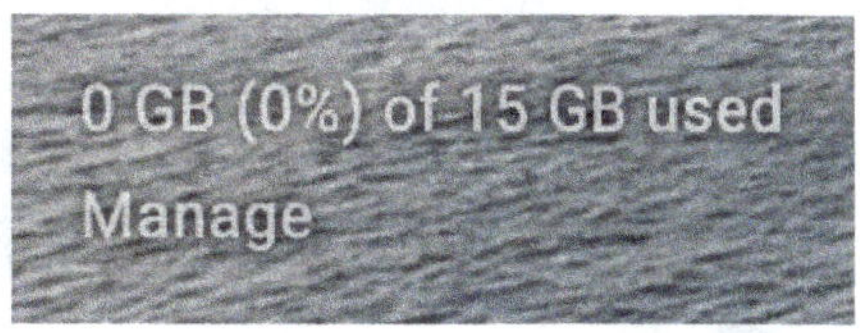

To the far, lower right, you can see your account activity. This tells you all the sessions that are signed in. Let's say you went to a public library and forgot to sign out. Yikes, right?! Go here and just click Details:

If there's a remote session in place—meaning someone is using your account from a distant place, then there's going to be an option to sign out. And speaking of signing out—how do you do that?! Go to the upper right corner. If you have a profile picture, then it will show your beautiful face. If not, it will have your abbreviation. When you click on that, you can Sign out:

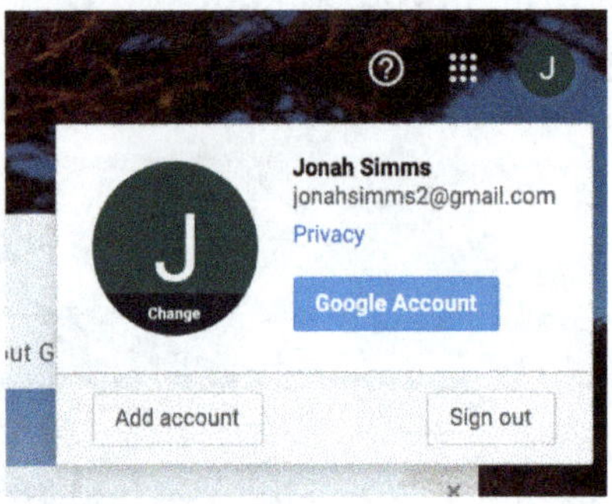

Next to that is a button with nine dots. Click that and you'll see some of Google's most popular apps. Since you have gmail, you have access to all of them:

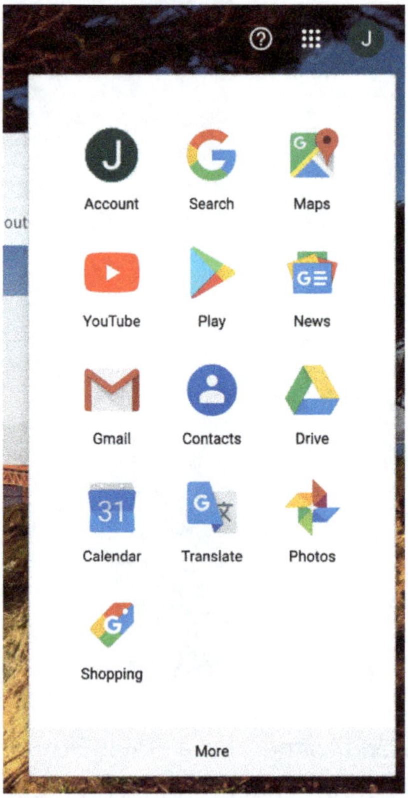

Just below that, you'll see a configure button. This is where you can do things like change the theme we set up earlier. We are going to spend a lot of time in this area. For now, just know where it is:

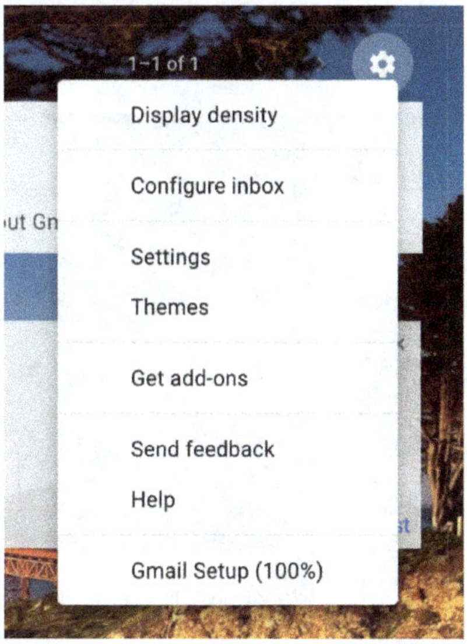

On the right side is the side menu. Here, you can get to your calendar, your idea book, your tasks, or you can add Gmail plugin apps (i.e. third party apps that tie into Gmail):

Finally, at the top is the search menu. This is where you can search your mail:

Near the bottom of your inbox, you'll see a 10% setup progress. What does that mean? You have email! Aren't you all setup?! Technically, yes. This is Google's way of helping you learn the email ropes. It actually is helpful, and you can do it very quickly.

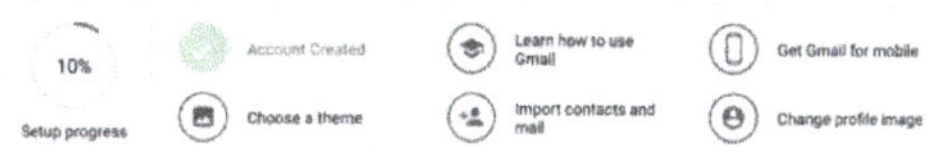

The first option is theme:

Theme puts an image on your inbox to make it a little more personal. Go ahead and pick one! Even if you haven't hit save yet, you'll see a preview:

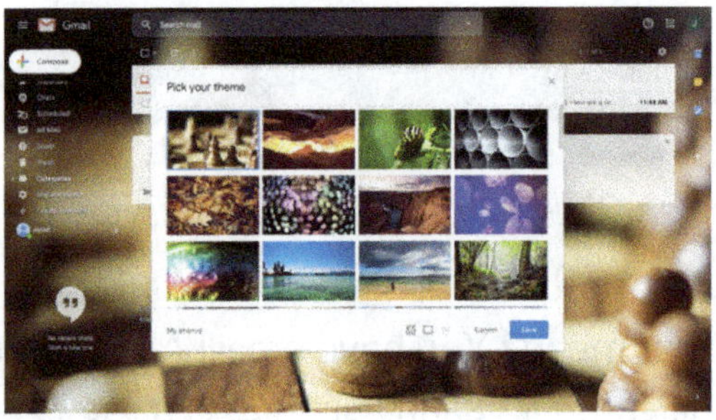

There are a few options on the bottom to help make the image easier to see behind your email. The first (the A button) makes the email area either dark or light. (You can change all of this later!)

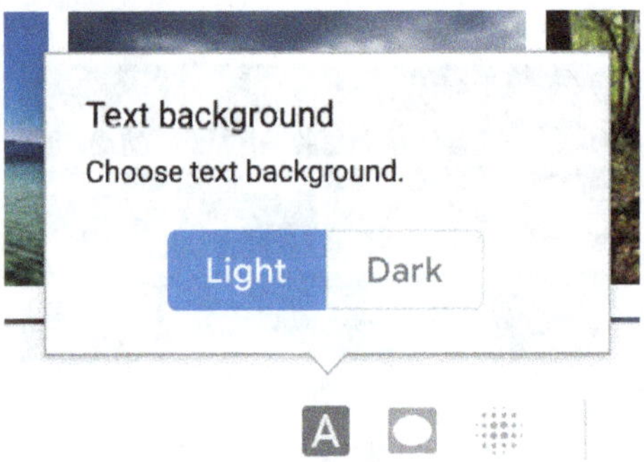

When you toggle it, you'll notice the background of your email is changing:

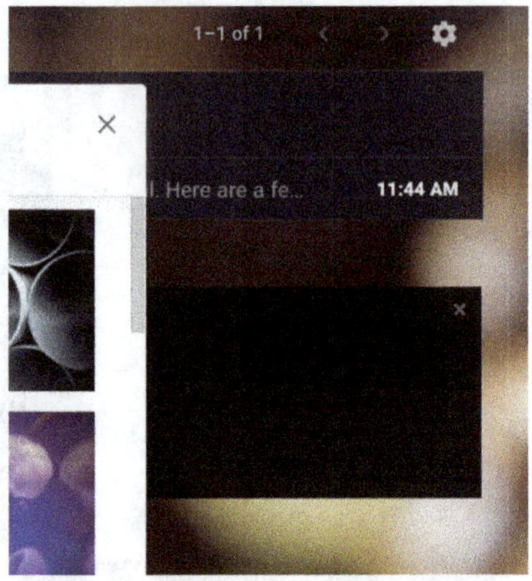

Next is vignette, which just makes the corners of the image darker. Sliding it to the right will adjust the darkness:

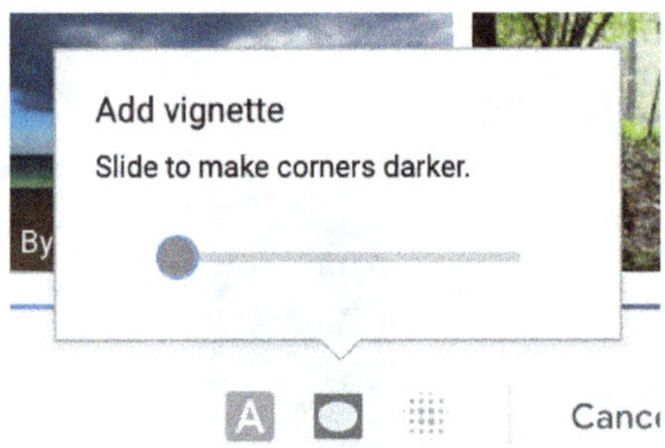

Finally, you can apply a blur. Personally, I like this feature best; when you have a really sharp image, it can make it harder to see text on the screen. Blurring the image makes emails and text stand out more, in my opinion.

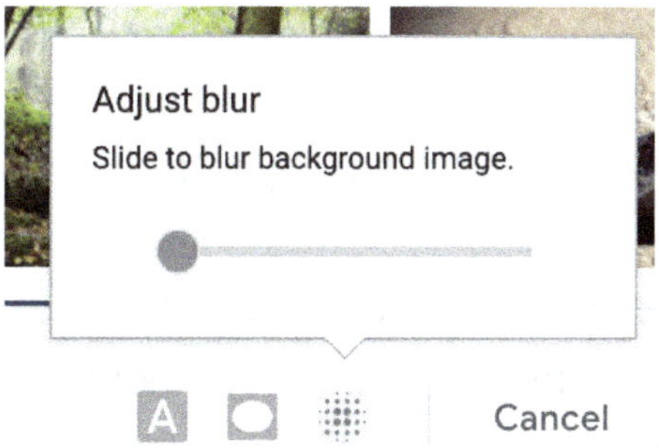

Once you hit save, you'll notice that this event is not done. You are one step closer to completing Gmail's quick setup!

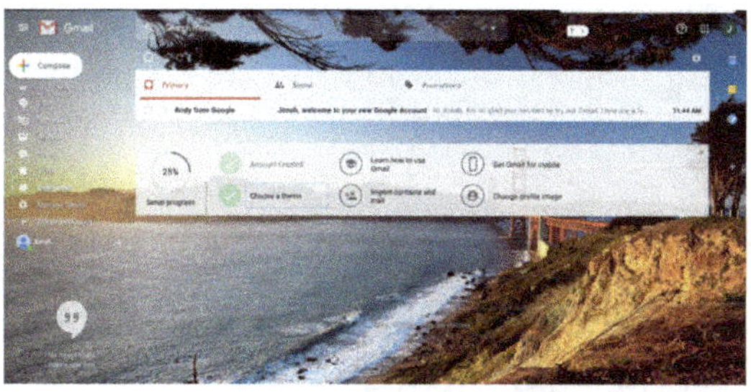

The next option is Learn how to use Gmail. Click on that and it brings up a help box. I do recommend spending a few seconds here. It has some good tips.

Close it and the activity is done!

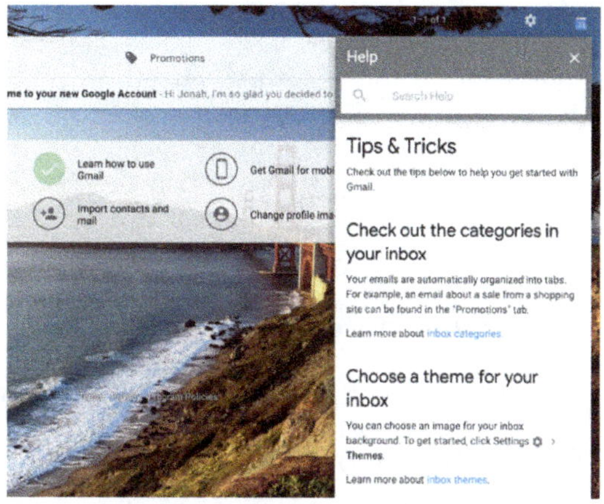

If you already have an email (such as a work email) and you want to import over all the contacts, click the Import contacts option; if you just want this to show that you've completed the setup, then click it and then cancel it:

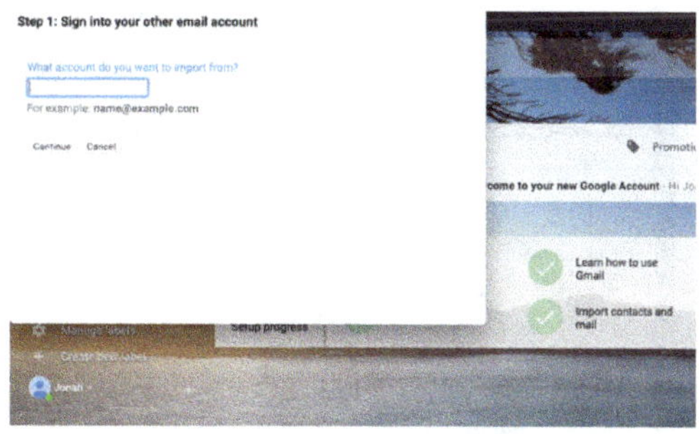

This is going to walk you through the quick and easy steps to connecting the email. In most cases, it's just a matter of signing into your email:

Getting the mobile app is next. The mobile app lets you read email on your phone or tablet—you can also get a mobile-friendly version of Gmail by going to Gmail.com from your browser. Using a native app, however, let's you get notifications of new mail in real time:

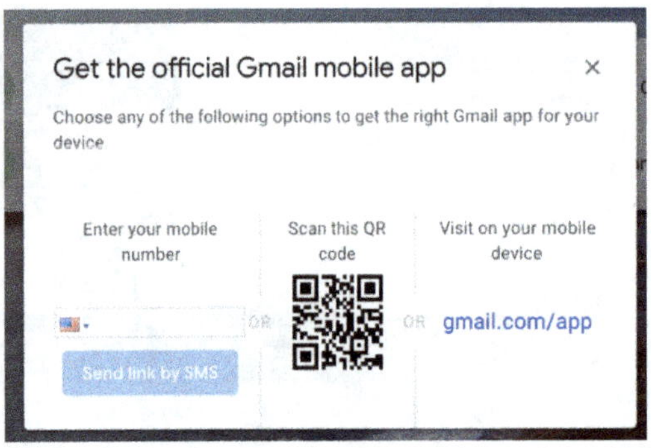

Next, select a profile photo. This is what people see when they get a message from you. You don't have to pick one, but I do recommend it. Sometimes people don't know who you are until they see your face:

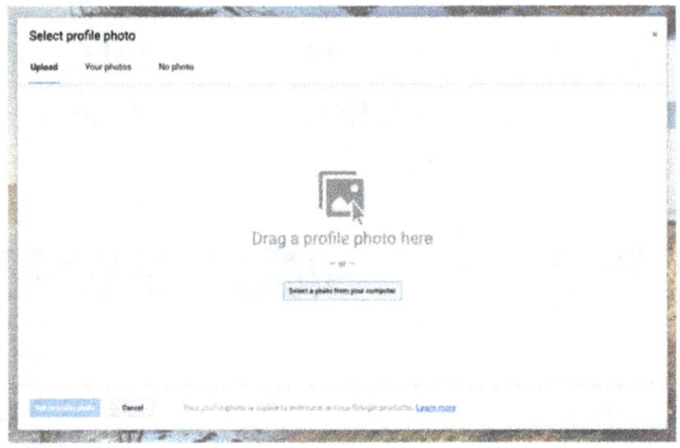

Once you complete that, you'll get the 100% badge of honor!

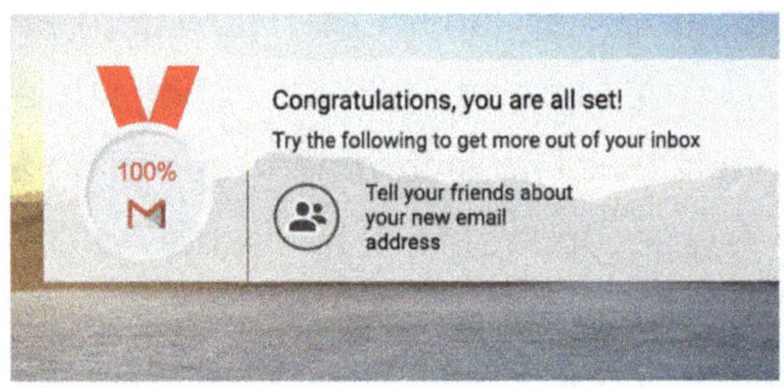

CHAPTER 2: HOW TO SEND AND RECEIVE MAIL

How to Send Email

Now that you know your way around, let's have some fun and send an email.

Email comes naturally for most people. But there's more inside the email then just compose and send. There's a lot of extra formatting you can do.

In case this is your first time using Gmail, or your first time using email, click the Compose button on the upper left hand side:

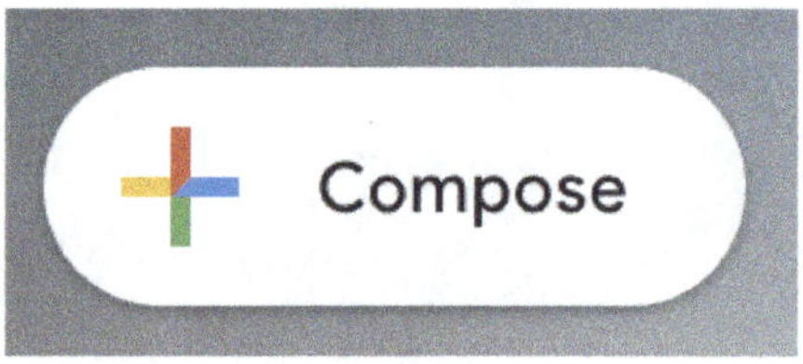

This opens up the New Message window:

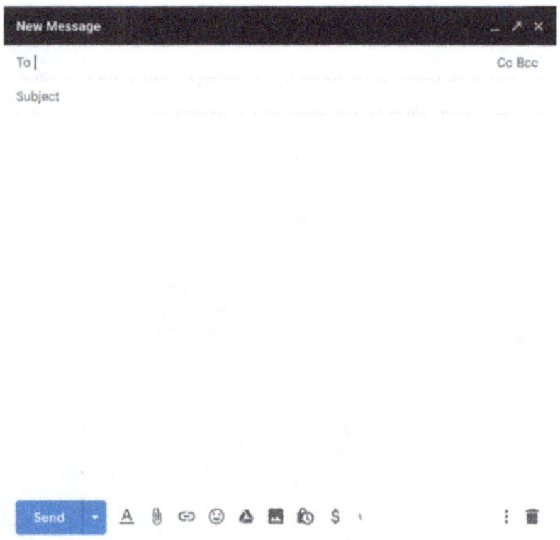

Click the arrow next to the X in the upper left corner. That makes the message larger; click it again to return to normal size:

By default, all you see is the "To" field. Enter someone's email here; if you want to send a CC or BCC, then click the button that says CC or BCC:

CC is a carbon copy—a copy of the email that will go to a person that you think needs to see the email, but does not necessarily need to reply. A BCC is a blind carbon copy. This means other people cannot see who you sent it to. If you are sending a huge list, one hack is to send it to yourself and BCC everyone else. This way everyone gets what you are sending, but they can't see everyone else on the list.

When you start typing in the body, you'll see the format bar. If you don't see it hit the A next to Send. You can add emojis to the subject, but you can't change the formatting here—for example, you can't Bold the subject.

The non-format menu is at the bottom of the message. I already said what "A" does. The paperclip attaches a file, the one next to that inserts a link into the message (you can also highlight a word and do CTRL+K for this), the face inserts an emoji, the triangle is Google Drive (if you have a file you want to attach that's in Google Drive versus your computer), next to that is to insert a picture, and finally, the little button with the clock puts the email in confidential mode.

Confidential mode is James Bond for email! This message will self-destruct kind of stuff! It takes away the ability for the person to forward, print, or copy the message. You can also set limits on when it expires, and require a code.

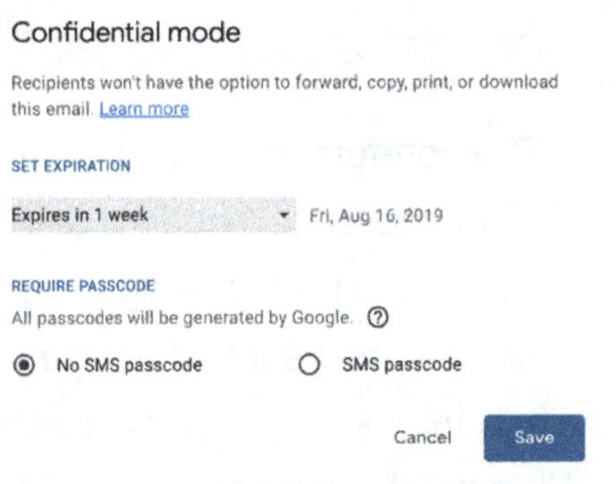

Finally, the money key lets you either send money via email or ask for money. You just need to add a debit card. It's kind of like Google's version of PayPal, but without the fees:

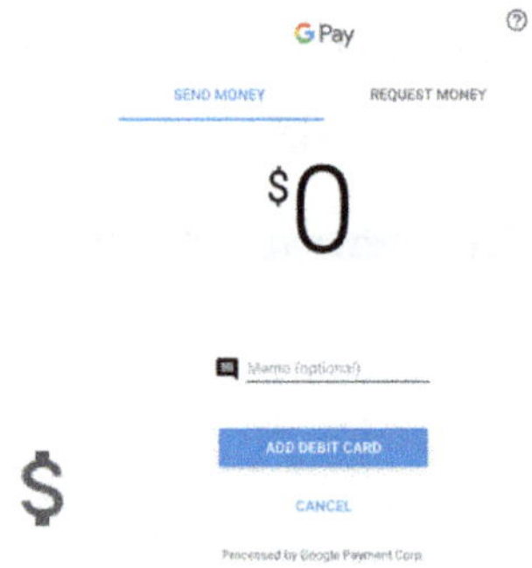

The three dots in the bottom left corner opens up the email menu; this lets you do things like spell check and print. You can also add a label, which we'll cover more in the next section.

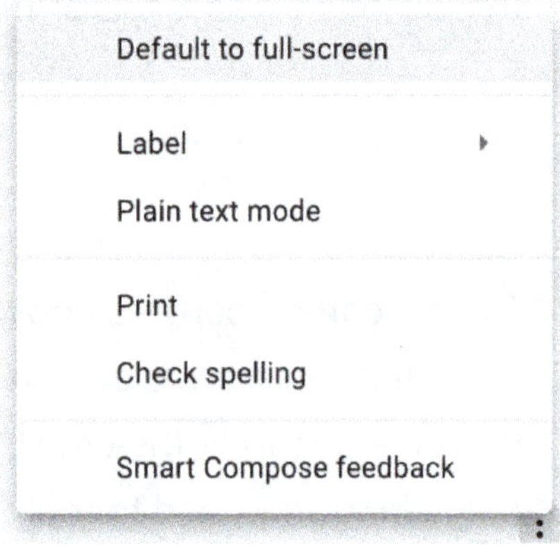

Finally, the trash icon deletes the message:

If you accidently close the message (or if you do it on purpose), go to that side menu and select Drafts. It will be there waiting for you. Just click it and the email will reopen.

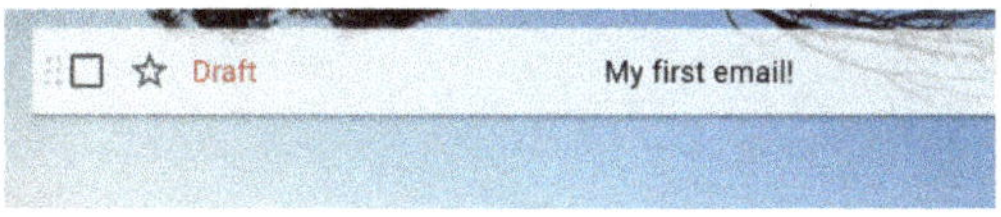

When you are ready to send the email, click the blue Send. If you want to schedule it (so it sends later), then just hit the arrow next to it:

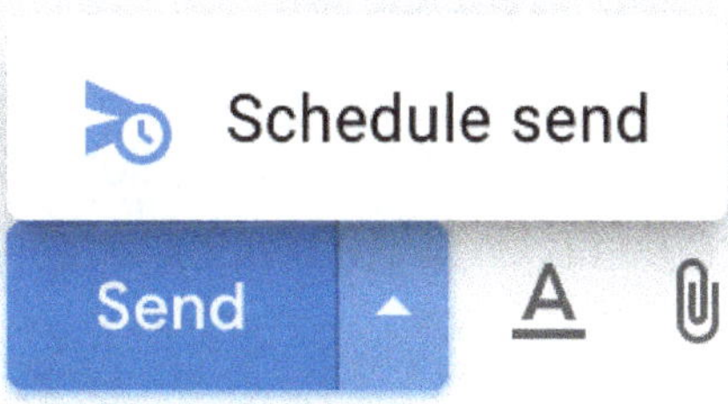

Google will show you common times to schedule it:

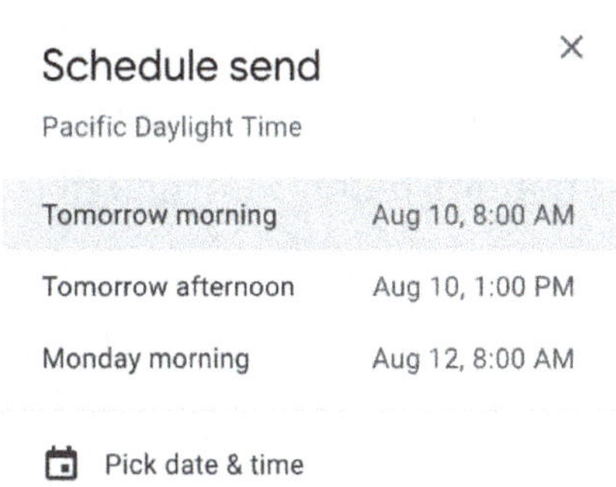

If those times don't work, then select Pick date & time, which opens up a calendar:

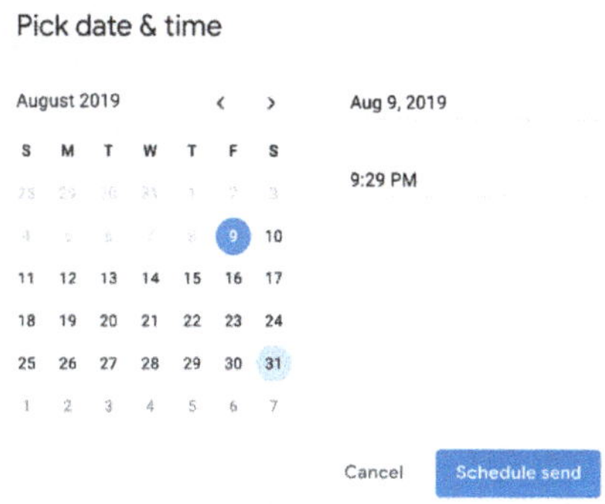

How to Read Email

A lot of people get an email, open an email, and reply to email. Sound familiar? There's so much more you can do to organize your inbox and be more productive.

The inbox is that big area in the middle of your screen. If you just started, then you probably have an email from Andy from Google:

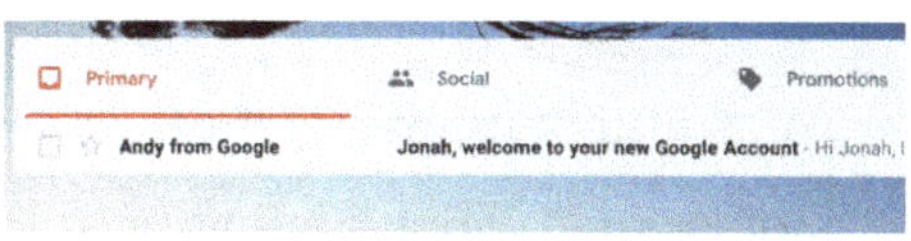

Above that are three tabs: Primary (where most of your email is), Social (friend requests and things pertaining to social networks), and Promotions (offers from companies you subscribe to). If someone swears up and down that they sent you an email and you don't see it in your Primary tab, then check Spam (in the menu to your left) or one of those tabs:

Not a fan of tabs and want to get rid of them? Or you are a fan and you want more? We are going to cover this soon when we talk about settings, but for now, click on Social. Near the bottom of your screen there's a message about the tab being empty, and how you can add or remove the tab. Click that blue inbox settings button:

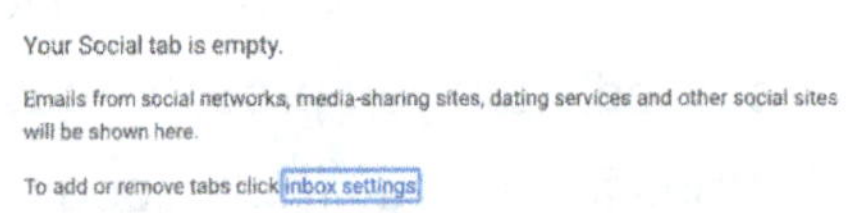

You'll notice there are three tabs with checkmarks. Those are your active tabs. You cannot uncheck primary, but you can check or uncheck anything else. Once you make your selection, hit the Save button:

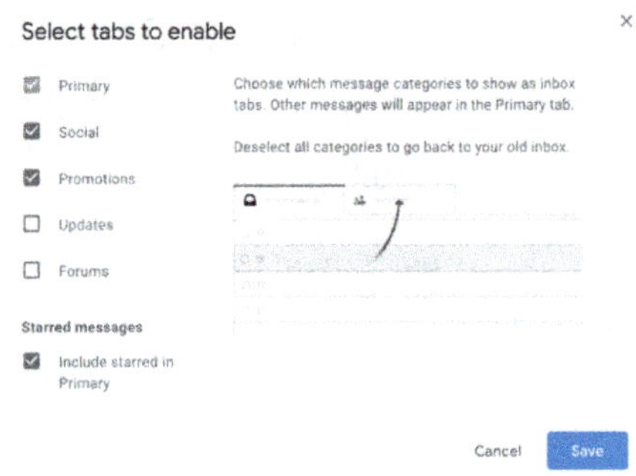

Click anywhere on the email you want to open. The top portion of the email is your main menu. The first button (the arrow) will get you back to your inbox; you can also get there by clicking on the Inbox link on the left menu. These menu options are also available in your Inbox when you click the check box on any of the messages:

The first three buttons on the menu are the email options. Let's say you've read the email—now what? You can either archive it (the down-arrow button), report it as junk (the ! button), or delete it (the trashcan button). If you don't do any of these three things, then the email will remain in your inbox. If you archive it, it will go to the folder marked All Mail—it will no longer show in your inbox. If you mark it as junk, then it goes in the folder marked Spam, which is eventually emptied automatically if you don't do it. If you delete it, it goes to your Trash folder, but, like Spam mail, it's not gone for good. You have thirty days to remove it.

If you accidently delete something or mark it as Spam, then go to the folder (either Spam or Trash), check the box next to the email, and select the button with the folder and right arrow:

Once you press that, it will ask you where you want to move the email to:

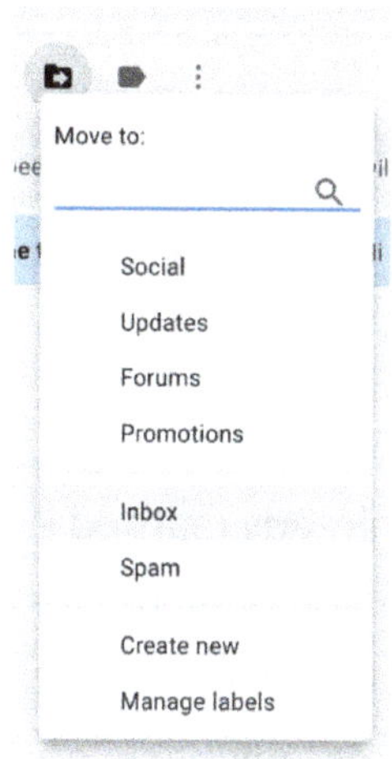

When you return to your inbox, you'll notice that the email is no longer bold. That's because it's been read. If you select the button with the mail symbol on it, it will mark it as unread. If you press the button with the clock, it will snooze it. Snooze means it will move it out of your inbox for a set period of time, and then move it back in at its designated time. I use this feature a lot for reservations and appointments. I schedule those emails to move back into the inbox on the day of the event, so it's easy to find. If you snoozed a message, but want to unsnoozed it, just go into the Snooze folder and follow the steps above for moving trash back into the inbox.

You already learned what the next button does—it moves the mail to another folder. Just like you can move trash or junk back into your inbox, you can also add new mail into another folder. The last button is the Label button:

Adding Labels

When you click the label button, it shows you all the labels already created. If you want to create a new one select Create New (you can also go into Manage Labels to edit or delete one that you have already created):

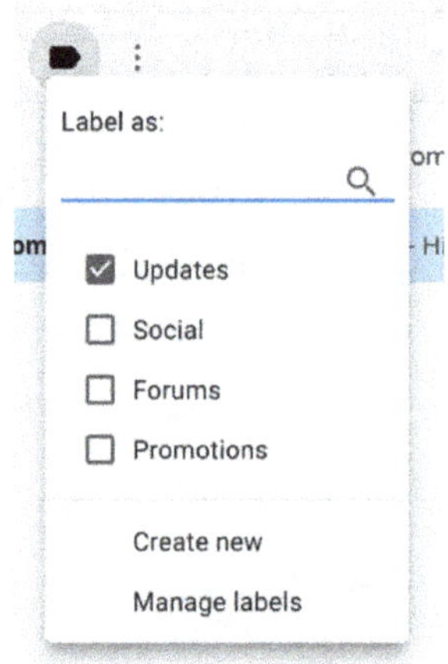

Next, enter the name. There's an option to "Nest a label under:" This doesn't work until you have created at least one custom label (those four that Google created don't count).

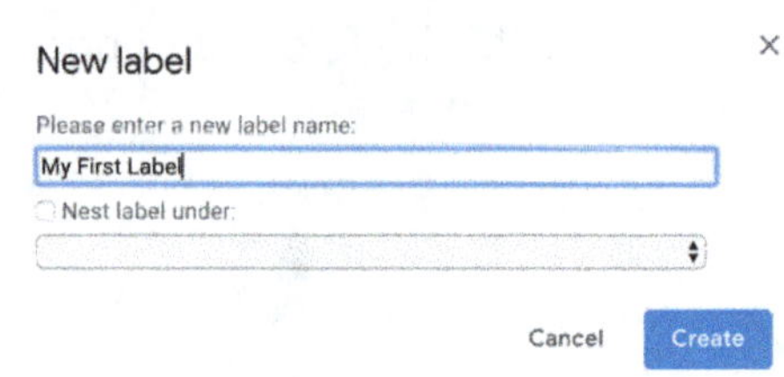

Once it's created, return to your inbox and you'll see the email now has the label name next to it:

You can see all messages with that label by clicking on the label from the left menu:

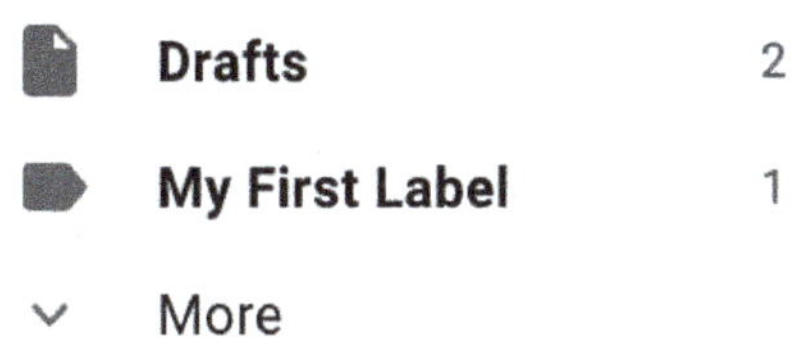

More Email Options

At the end of the menu is the button with three dots. This brings up some of the less commonly used features. We will cover most of them later in the book:

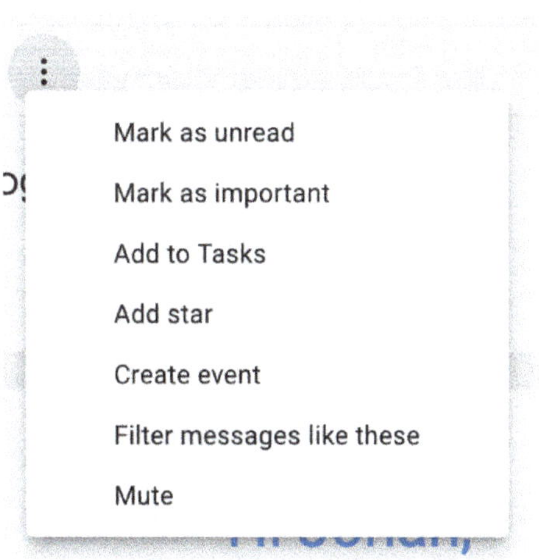

The 1 of 1 (it varies depending on the number of emails you have) with the arrow keys lets you go through emails without going back to the inbox. The right arrow takes you to the next email and the left goes back to the previous:

The keyboard changes the language of the email. This is helpful if you are replying to an email in another language. Click Input Tools Settings and you'll see dozens of different languages:

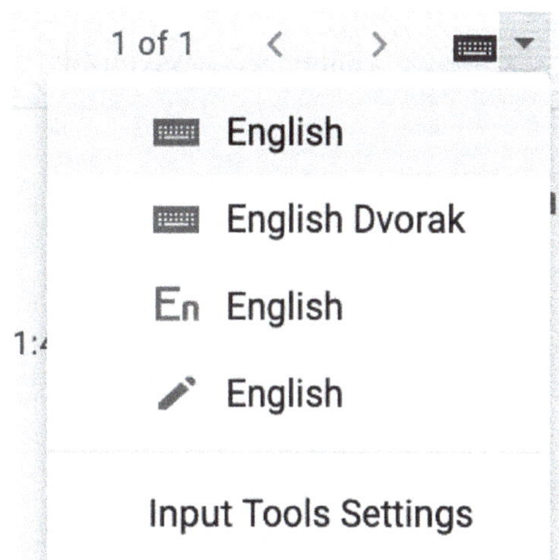

The Configure button will be discussed as we get to each of these features:

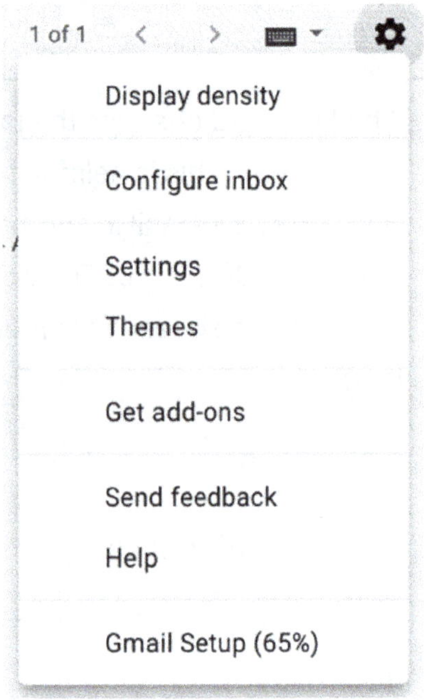

In the body of the email itself, there are a few things to note. First, if you hover over the sender's name, you can add them to your contacts, set up a calendar event with them, or email them a separate email:

On the right side of the message, there are several things you should note. The first is the time; this tells you when an email arrived (not when you opened it):

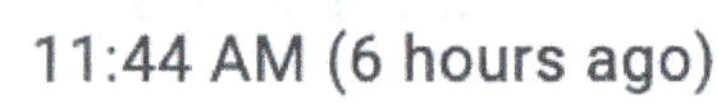

Next to that is the star. By default, all emails have no star. Stars help you organize your mail, and make important emails stand out. You can have a folder with 100 emails, and filter it by only Starred emails (which you should have less of).

Next to the star is the reply button:

And next to the reply is a button with three dots. This gives you a long list of different options—most you will never use:

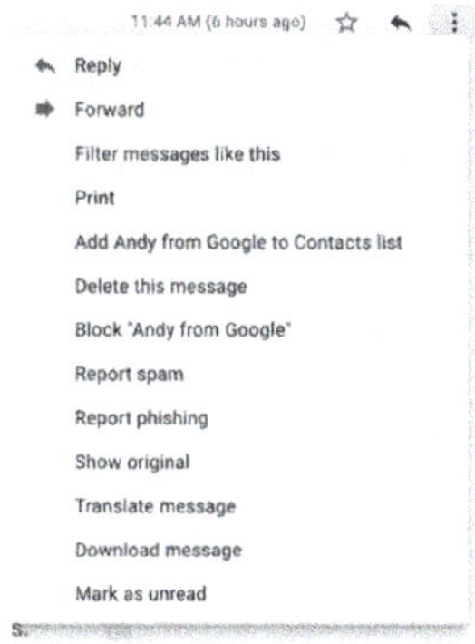

At the bottom of the email are two additional buttons: to Reply or Forward the message:

When you reply, it looks just like composing an email, but the person's name and the subject is already there, and the email is at the bottom of the original message—not like a popup box (as it is when you compose a new message):

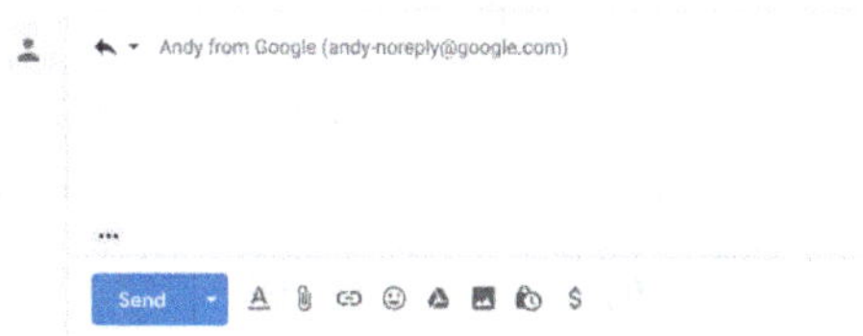

Forward looks similar, but there's a place to type in a recipient under "To":

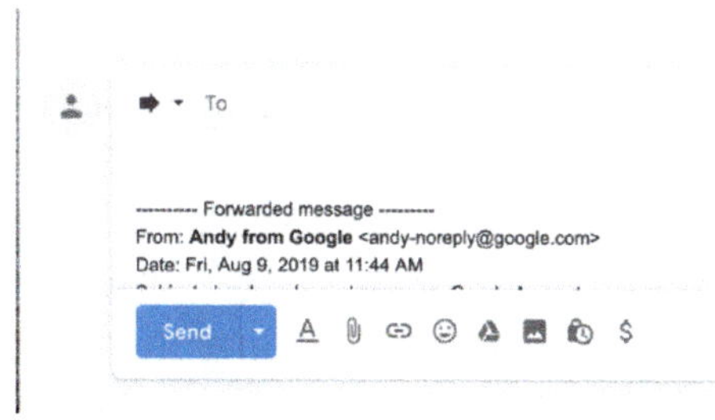

Adding Contacts

Now you are ready to email someone new. Go over to the side to your contacts. Where is it? Exactly! Gmail doesn't have a dedicated place for contacts in the app. When you type someone's name, it will predict what you are typing and pull the contact up. But how do you add a contact?

You have to go to a separate website: contacts.google.com. Here you can import, export, and lots of other things. We'll be focusing on the most important thing: adding a contact:

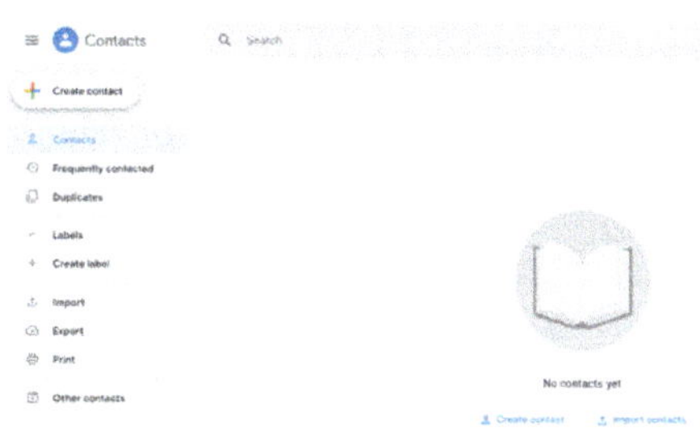

Click the Create contact button:

This gives you several things you can add:

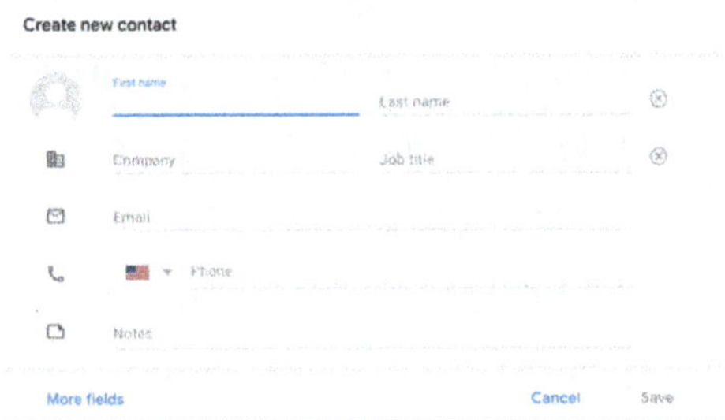

Not comprehensive enough?! Click More fields:

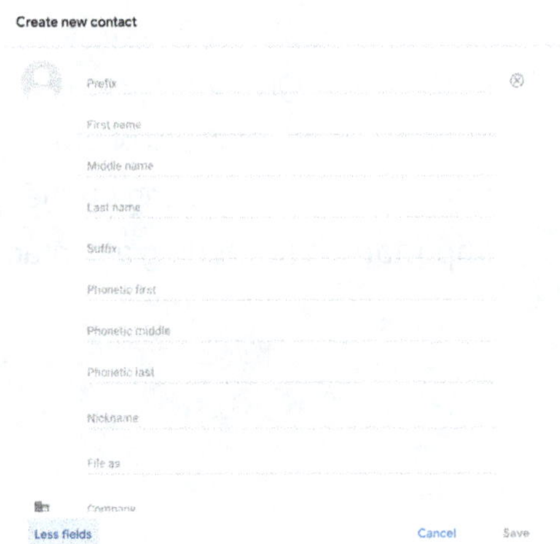

I'm going to add one for my very good friend with an unfortunate name: John Doe. I can create a label for him so I know if he's a work friend or family member:

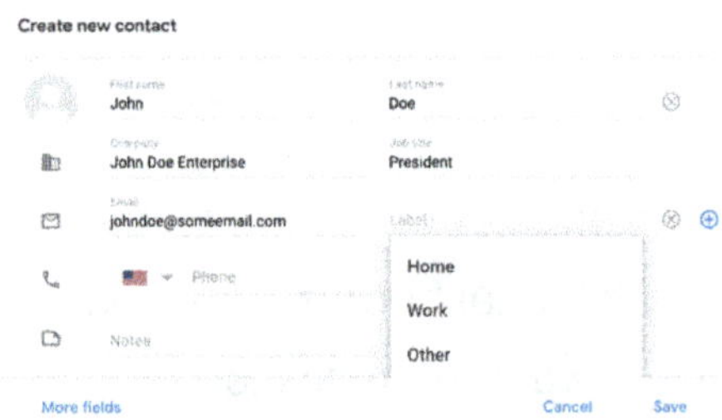

Once I save it and click his name from my contact list, it displaces everything you have inputted about good old John. You can even click on his email (I used Andy's from Google for this example) and it will open the email right up:

Searching Mail

Finding email is pretty easy with Google. You can simply search for a keyword like "budget":

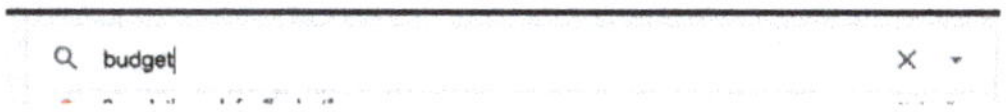

Or you can click the arrow next to the search box and have more details. You can search for the word "Budget" but tell Gmail that you only want to see emails from a certain person, sent on a certain date, and it included an attachment:

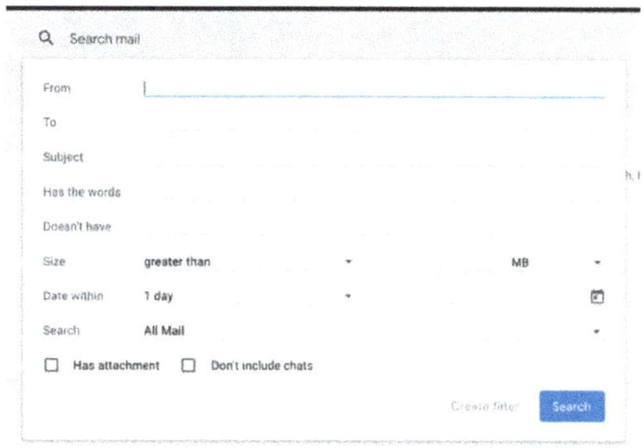

CHAPTER 3: CHATS AND PHONE / VIDEO CALLS

Email is cool, but today people are all about real-time answers. That's where Google Chat and Hangouts become important.

These tools are both in the same place. Chat is like an instant message and Hangouts is a video call. To get started with either, go to Start a new one below the conversations icon:

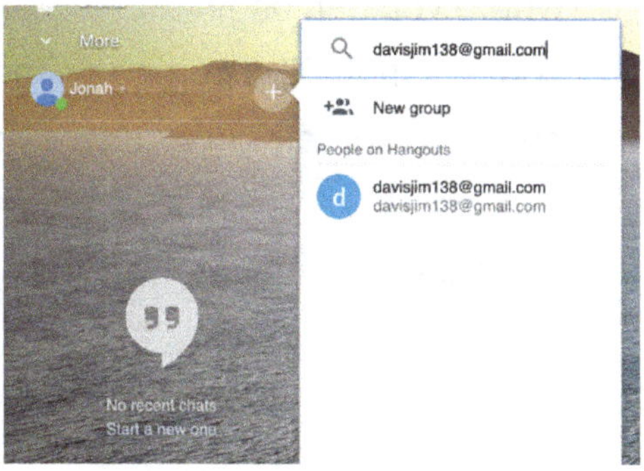

After your first Hangout, it will show you've had a conversation already:

To start a new one, just click the + sign as in the image below:

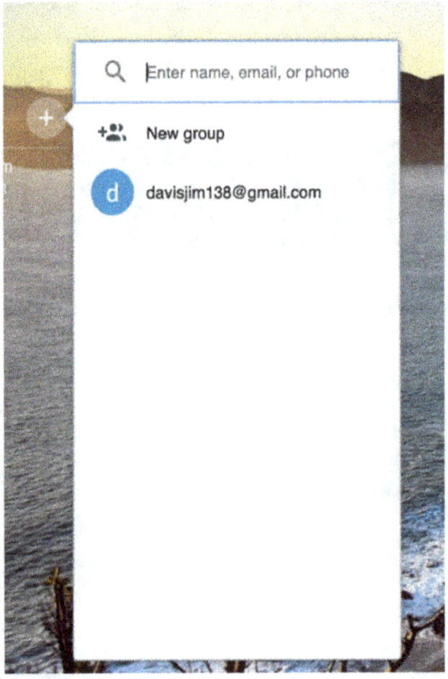

You can also bring this up with the menu bar on the very bottom left side of your screen. Here, I'll point out one icon you should know: the phone:

When you click that, you can make a free phone call right from your browser! There's not a lot to it, so I won't cover it in detail. Add the number you want and hit enter. That's it! When a person gets the call, it will say unknown. If you want your own personal Google number, then hit the + next to the $0.00. It will walk you through the steps to get a number. Why does it say $0.00 if it's free? Because it's only free within the U.S. and Canada. If you call outside that, there is a cost—albeit a low one. Some countries cost $0.01 a minute, some more remote, undeveloped countries cost over $1 a minute.

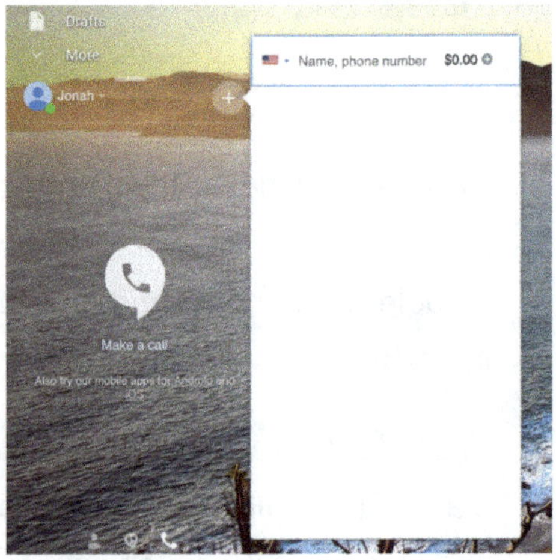

Back to Chat/Hangout; once you type in a valid email, it will open a box where you can begin the conversation. The person on the other end sees something similar. Type your message where it says Send a message, and hit enter/return:

Want to do a group chat? Click the icon of a person with a +, then add the person's email:

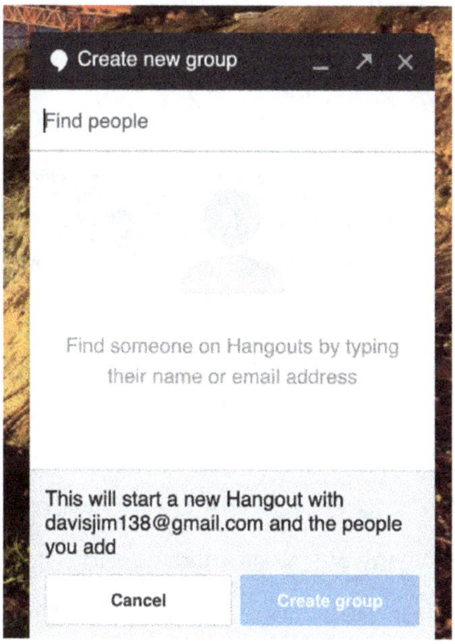

The configure button has several options such as if you want to archive or delete the conversation (if you delete it, then you won't be able to recover it):

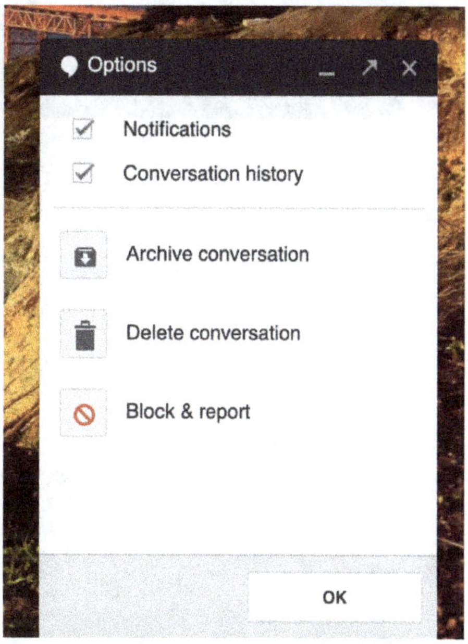

To start a Hangout, click the camera button. This opens a separate window. If it's your first Hangout, it's going to ask for a few permissions. Basically, Google is asking your computer if it's okay to use your webcam and mic:

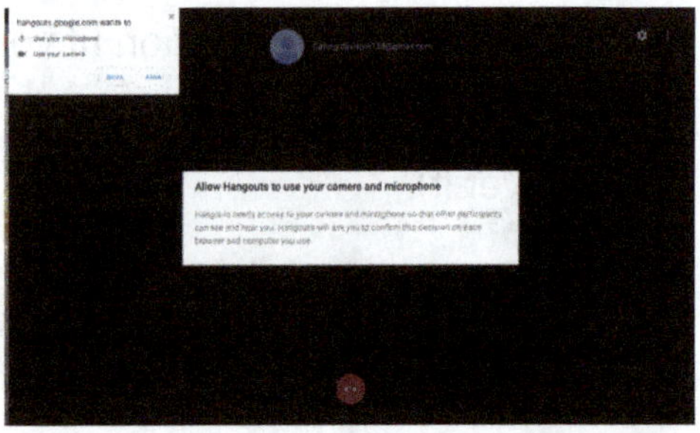

As you're getting set up, the other person will see a notification in Gmail saying someone wants to video call them:

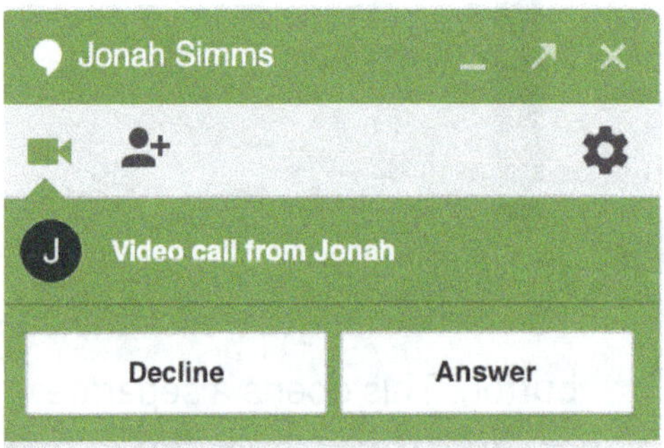

If you didn't set up your camera or mic, you can still do it while you are on the call. Just click the configure button in the upper right corner.

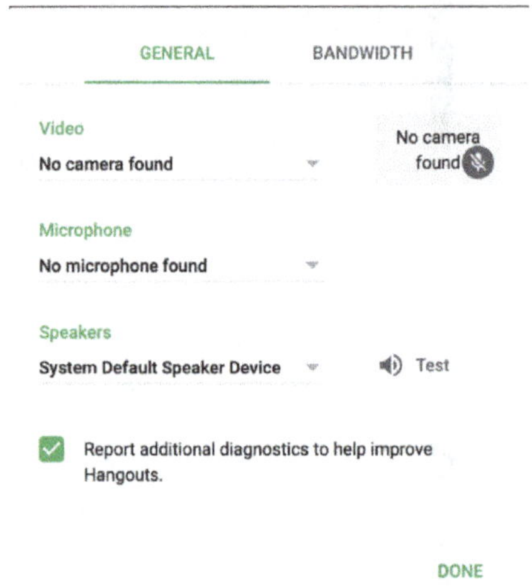

In the bottom left corner, there's an option to send messages. This is like the Chat we just saw. It's helpful if you are sending links while you are on the call:

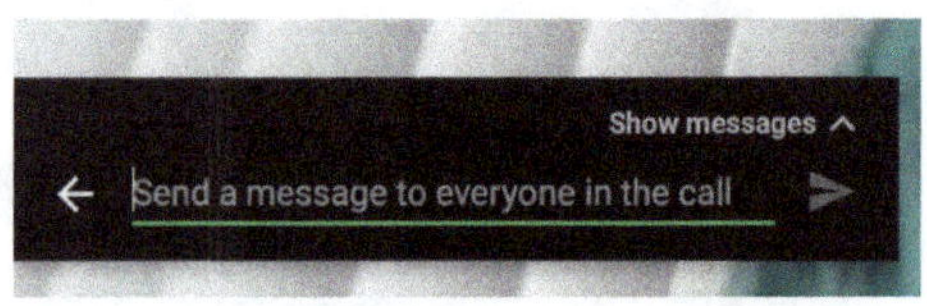

In the upper right corner, you'll see three dots; this brings up the Hangouts option. These are pretty self-explanatory, but one in particular that you should know about: Share screen. Share screen lets the person on the other end see what's on your screen. This is very helpful when you are troubleshooting a problem with someone.

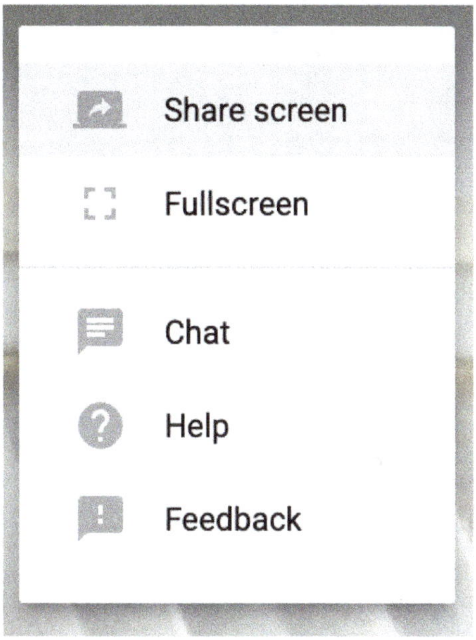

If you want to invite someone else into the hangout and have a group call, click on the person icon. It's similar to adding someone to a group text. Just add their email. You can also copy a link to the Hangout and share it. Anyone with the link can get in after you approve them.

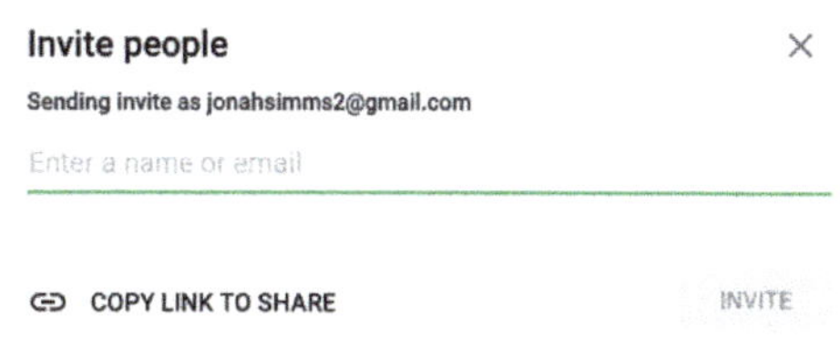

Finally, on the middle of the screen is where you go to hang up; in this section, you can also turn off your Mic or Webcam. If you are in a group Hangout, it's best to leave your mic off when you aren't speaking. It often picks up noises and Google will think your speaking and switch the camera to you.

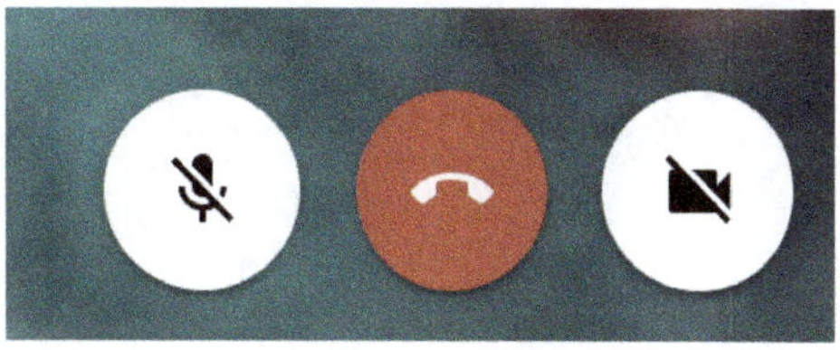

Chapter 4: Settings

Settings is where you go to customize your Inbox even more. We've already covered several things found here; I'll quickly reference it again where applicable.

Because this is a simple guide, I'm going to skim over some of the more advanced features that you probably won't be using; I'll cover them in case it's a topic you want to further investigate later.

To get started, click the configuration button on the righthand side of your email:

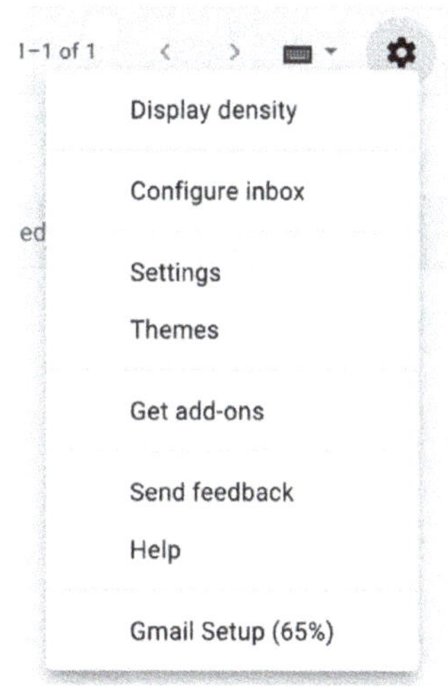

Display density was one of the first things covered in this book. This is how your inbox looks—compact with attachments not shown, for example:

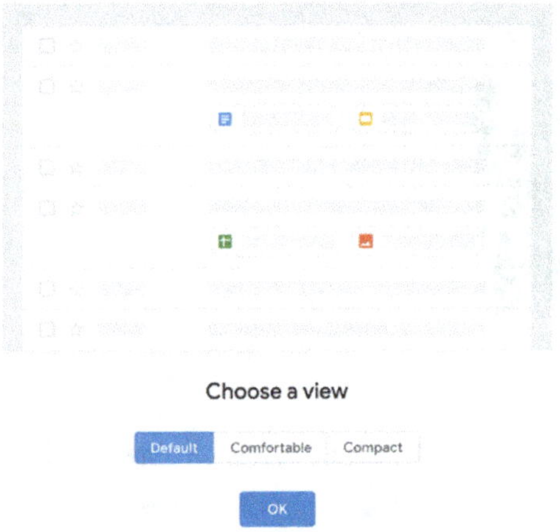

Configure inbox is where you turn those tabs on and off:

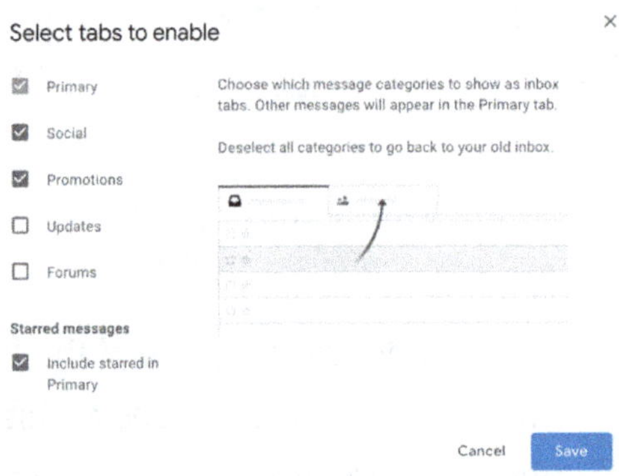

Skipping down a little, Themes is where you pick the background for your inbox:

Gmail setup is that little bar we saw on the bottom of our screen when we first started Gmail; mine went back to 65% because I merely opened the setting, but didn't change it. It doesn't really matter—Gmail doesn't behave differently because you are not at 100%.

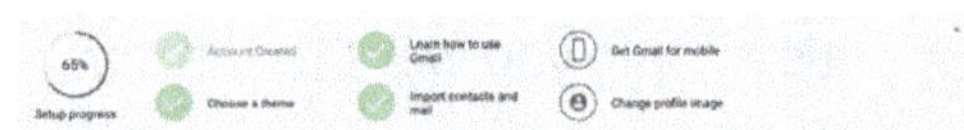

Settings is where we will spend the biggest chunk of our time in this chapter. When you click Settings, you'll see a menu at the top of your Inbox with a lot of options.

Let's start with the first menu: General. This is where you'll change things like the language and the style of your emails. There's a lot here you will not use. We'll look at some of the things you might use.

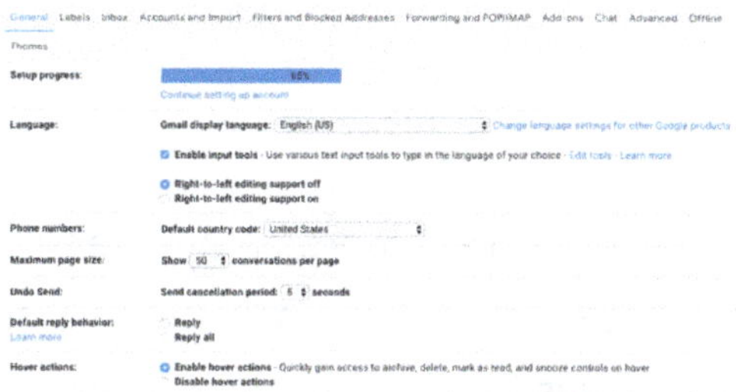

Default text style is the font, font size, and font color you use in your email. Let's say you love the color red and want big fonts. You could manually change this for every email you send, but you can also make the change here and every email you send will have that style.

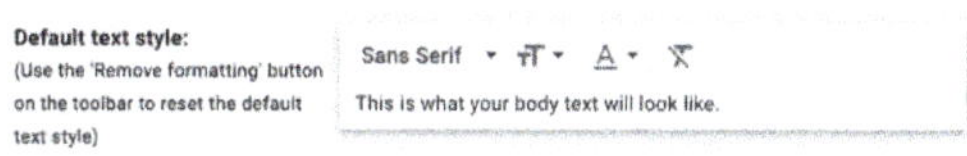

Conversation View is on by default. It groups all similar email topics together and makes it easy to follow conversations; if you aren't a fan, then turn it off here:

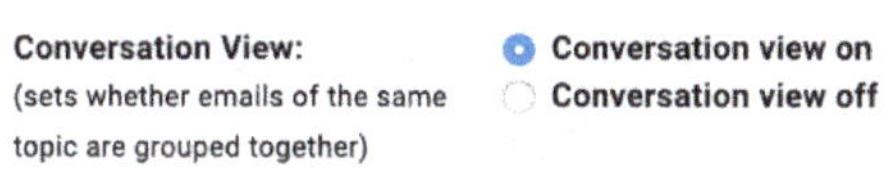

Nudges is also on by default. If an email needs a reply and you haven't done it, Nudges will automatically move it to the top of your inbox after a set number of days.

Smart reply is a somewhat new feature. A Google bot gives you a reply that it thinks is appropriate. So let's say someone emails you, "Here's the doc that you wanted." The suggested reply would probably be, "Thanks!" It would show the text in grey, and hitting the tab button will add it:

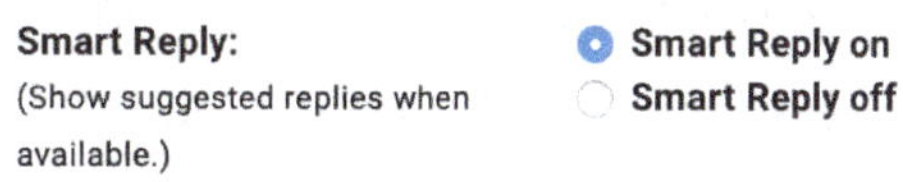

Desktop notifications allows Gmail to send you alerts on your desktop/laptop saying that you have a new email or other notification:

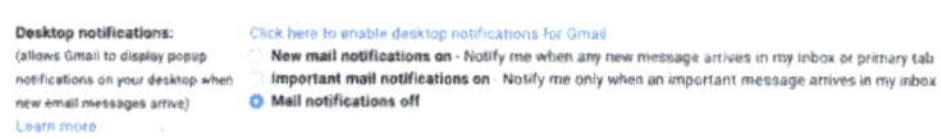

Signature is how you sign off on emails. That way if you always sign off:

Sincerely,

John Doe

111-111-1111

you could add that signature here, and every email would include it. You only see the signature after you send the email.

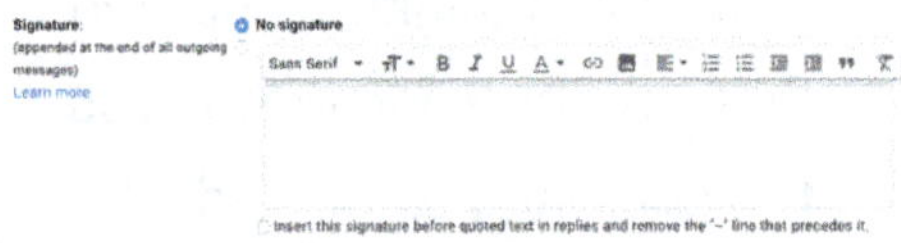

Vacation responder can automatically reply to emails saying you are away and won't be able to respond. You have to set the first day, but the last day is optional. If you don't set the last day, then make sure you come back in and turn it off when you are done with your vacation:

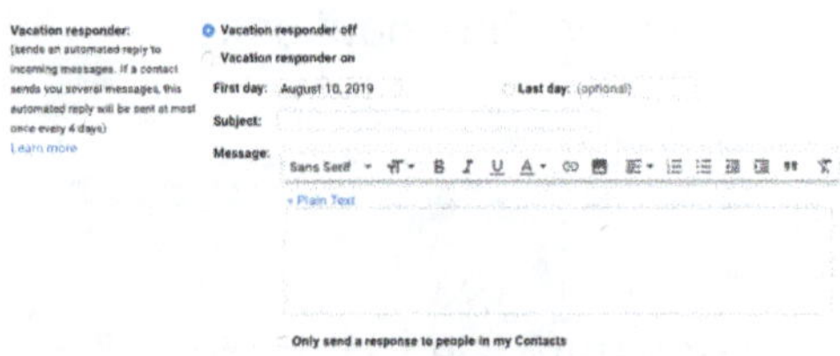

At the bottom is the Save Changes/ Cancel button; if it's greyed out, then no changes have been made. Note: some of these menus have the save options and others save automatically —make sure and look at the bottom before closing the menu.

Click on any word on the menu bar and it brings up a new menu. The next one is Labels. We've already covered this section, but this is how you get back to it.

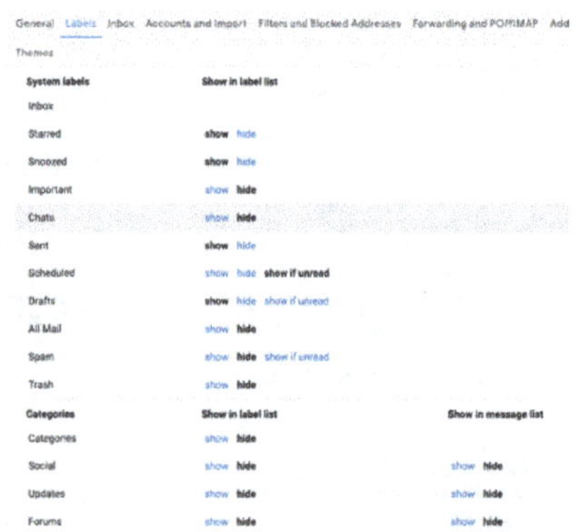

If you created a label earlier, then you should see it at the bottom of this setting:

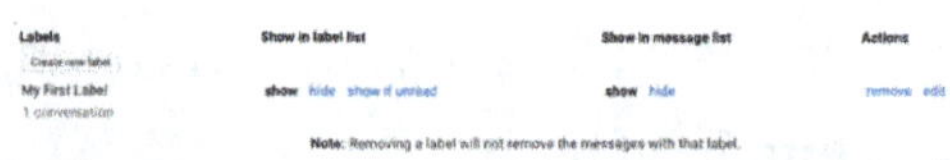

We've also seen many of the settings in the Inbox already.

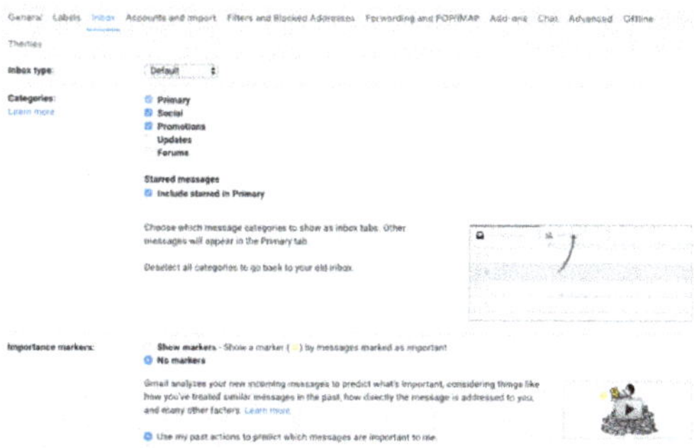

There is a setting at the bottom that changes the order of emails, for example, if you want to show unread first. That means you may have a newer email that you've already read that will be lower than an Unread one (or whatever you have selected):

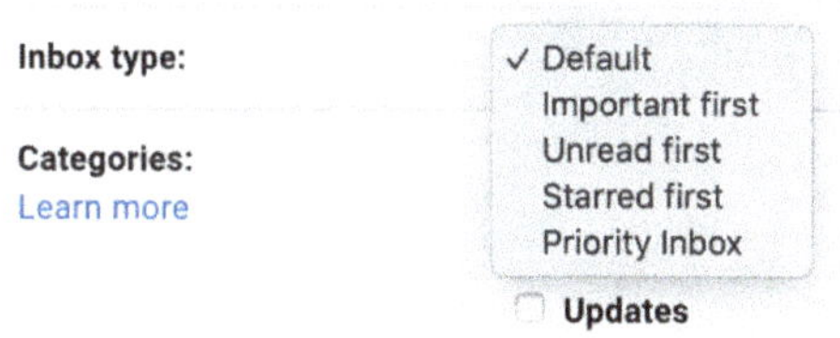

Accounts and Import is where you can go to change your email:

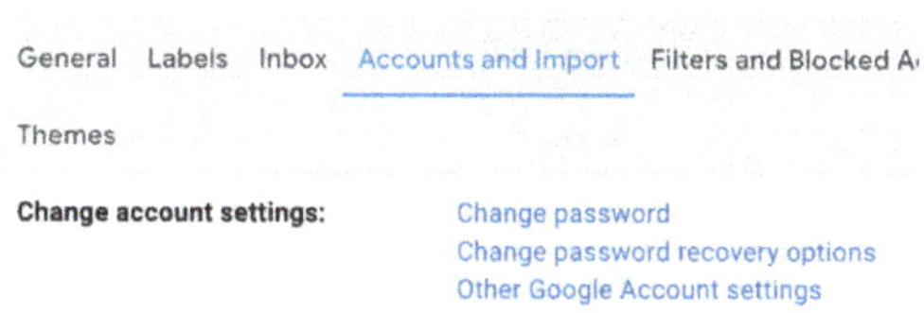

You can also change the name that you send mail as. So if you send mail as Jonah Simms, but want to send it instead as J Simms, then just click edit info on the right-hand side.

You can also add another email account in this setting. Just click Add a mail account. Why would you do this? Personally, I have several email accounts, and I have all mail forwarded to the main one. When I add other accounts, I can reply to them from my main account. So I have several accounts, but I never log into them. I have one for professional contacts; one for giveaways; one for family and friends.

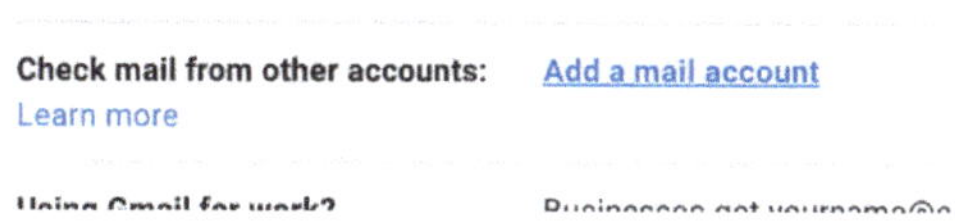

Filters and Blocked Addresses is where you go if there's someone you never want to speak to. You will still get messages from them, but they will go to your Spam. If the friend gets on your good side again, just go back and uncheck them.

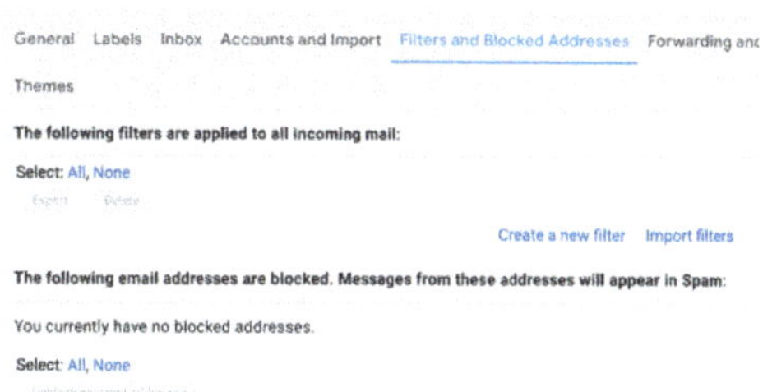

Forwarding and POP/IMAP get pretty technical. If you want to add a work email to Gmail, you can do it here, but you will probably need the IT guy's help in getting some of the settings. One thing you should know here is Forwarding. Forwarding lets you forward all of your email to another inbox. So let's say you want to give people another email so they don't know your main one; their email gets forwarded to your main one, so you don't have to keep checking this one.

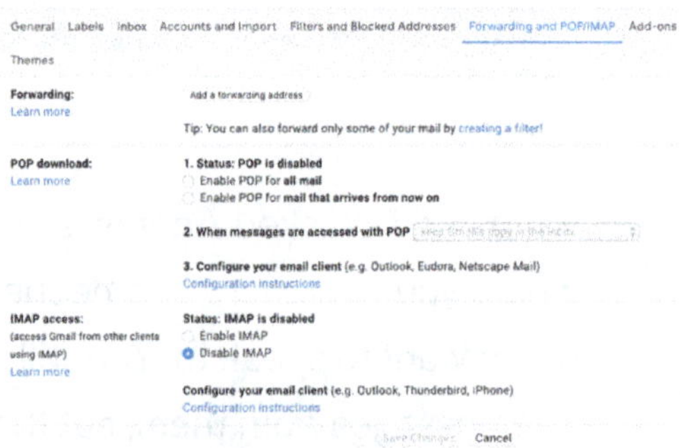

Add-ons will be covered in the next chapter. This is where you can add third-party apps:

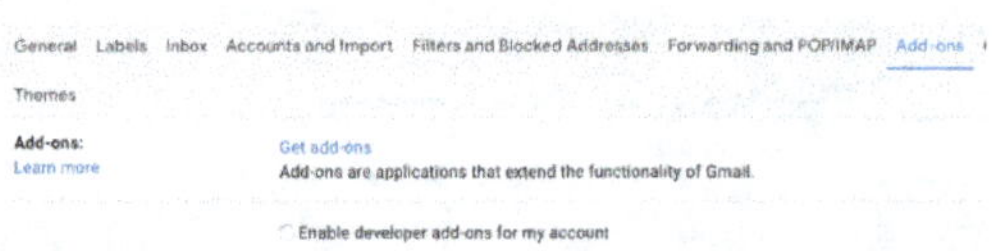

Chat is pretty straight forward. It turns the chat widget on the left side on and off:

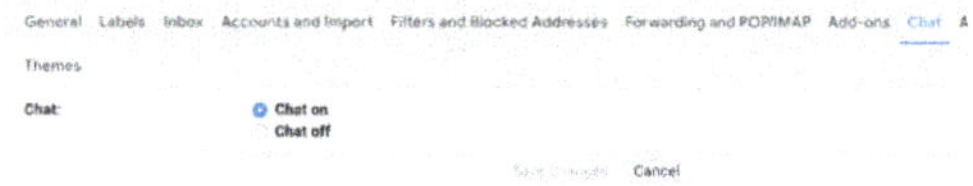

Advanced isn't as advanced as it sounds. By default, everything is disabled. If you want something turned on, just click Enable:

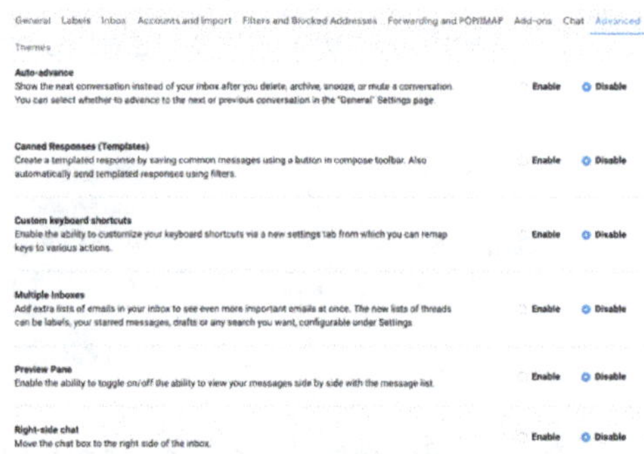

Finally, Offline lets you download your email to your computer:

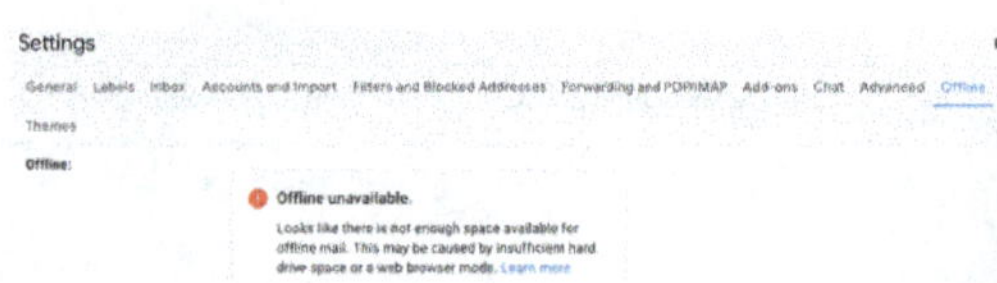

When you are ready to sign off for the day, click your profile photo or name in the upper right corner:

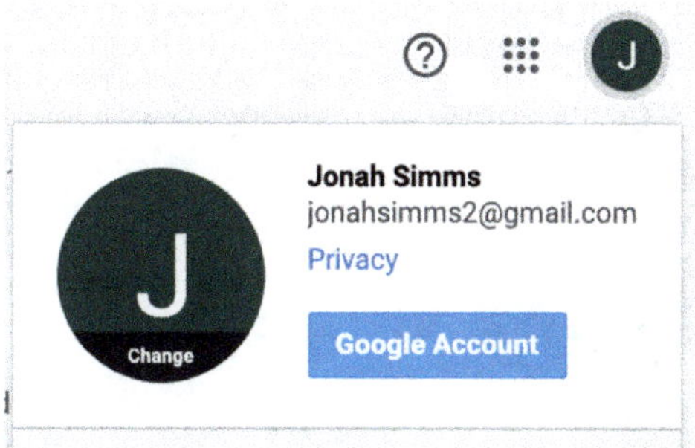

In addition to signing off, this is also where you can add additional accounts. So you can be signed in to multiple accounts and toggle between them.

Chapter 5: Calendar

The point of this book is to show you how to use your Gmail account; because a lot of your email is tied to the calendar, I'll give a very high-level overview of Google Calendar here. To get started, go to calendar.google.com. By default, it will give you a monthly view of your calendar:

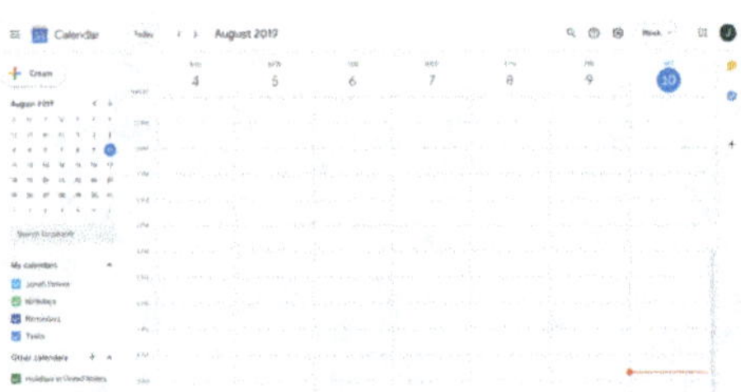

You can switch from monthly/yearly/ daily or any other views by clicking on Week over on the side; you can also go to the following months (or previous months) by clicking on the arrows next to the smaller calendar.

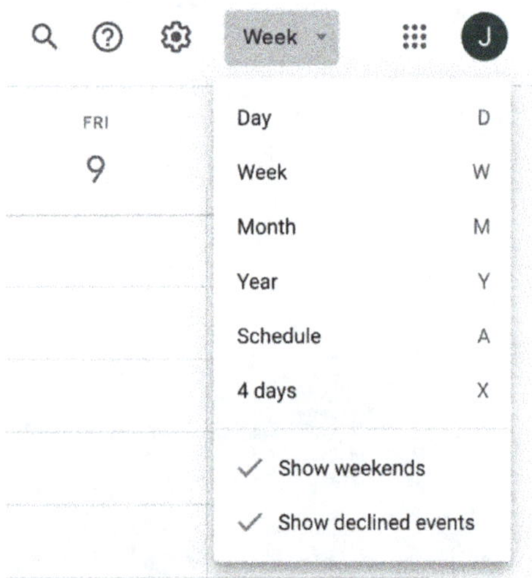

Over on the left side, just above "Holidays in the United States" is the option to add other calendars. For example, your spouse or sibling may have a calendar; they can share it with you so you can arrange appointments. This is frequently used in business when a manager needs to see an employee—they'll share their calendar and tell the employee to find an opening and create an event.

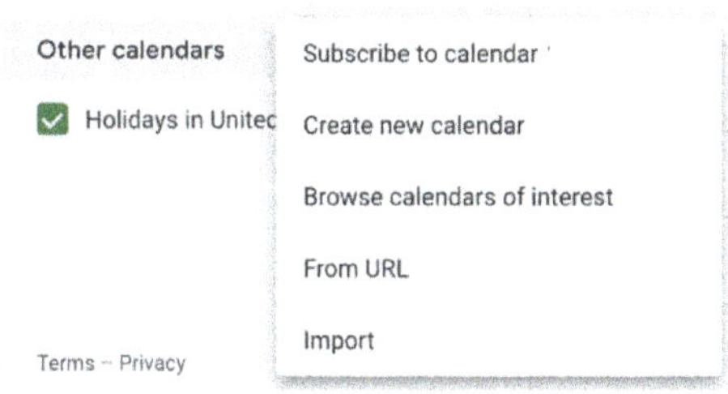

So how do you create an event? Click the big Create button over on the left side:

This brings up a small box that will ask you for the details. You can create it as a traditional event, or also as just a reminder or a task. You can also add a location and guests. If you add guests, they will need to accept your invitation:

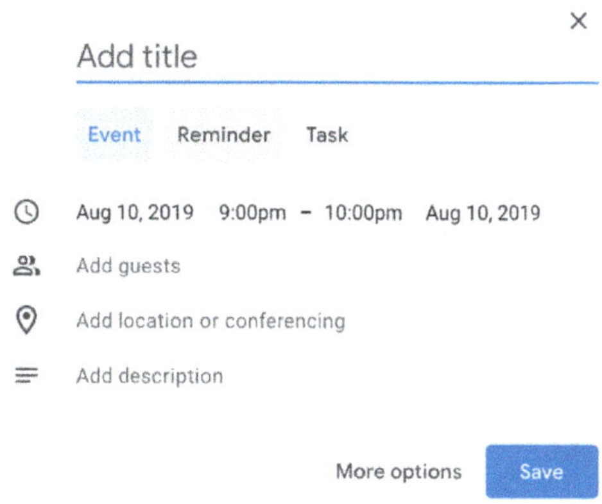

Clicking on More options, expands the box to show you even more things to add. This is what you would use if you want to attach something to the event (like the meeting minutes). You can also set up notifications, so you'll get an alert at a set time saying that the meeting is beginning.

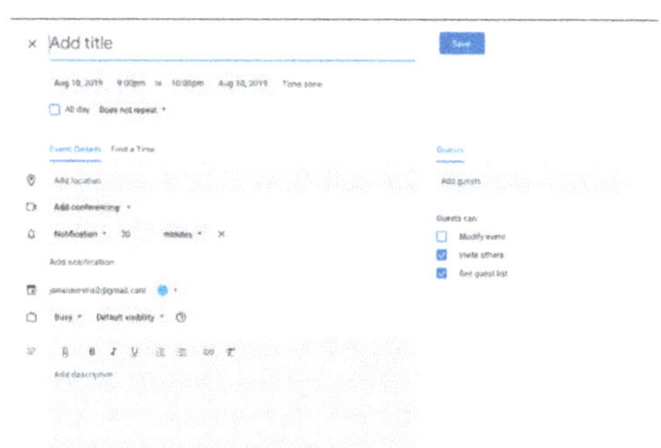

Chapter 6: Third Party Apps

There are hundreds and hundreds of third party apps for Gmail. In this book, I'm not going to cover the apps you should have. It's really a preference. I'm going to cover what they are in general and how to add them.

So what are they? Think of them like Add-ons. Dropbox (the cloud-based file locker), for example, has a third-party app that puts a Dropbox icon in your message box. You know when you are composing a message and you see that paperclip to attach a file? You'll also see a Dropbox icon to attach a file in Dropbox.

On the right side menu, click the + button:

This brings up a box that shows you all the possible apps you can add to Gmail (use at your own risk!); the first ones you see are the more popular apps:

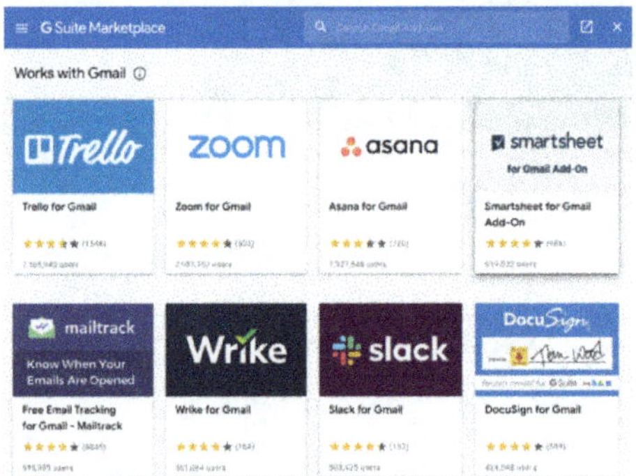

If you click the three lines in the upper left side, this lets you see all the different categories.

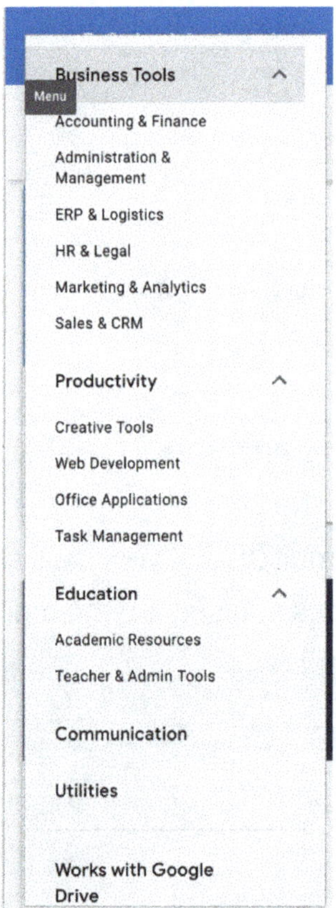

At the very bottom of the list is the Manage Apps option; that lets you remove or control the apps that you have already added:

Chapter 7: How To Cancel Gmail

Now that you've read all of this, what if you decide Gmail isn't for you? You have two options:

1. Don't log back in.
2. Manually delete it.

There's usually not a direct reason to delete your account. If you are worried someone will hack into something you never use, then that would be a reason—but Google, being Google, invests a lot of money into security.

The advantage of keeping it is you always have access to emails if you ever need them. Maybe one day you'll need something you never imagined you would need.

If you want to delete your account permanently, then head over here—and remember! There's no recovering email once you delete it, so be extra sure before you do this:

https://myaccount.google.com

Email has settings and your account has settings as well. This is sort of your master settings. It controls all Google Apps tied to your account:

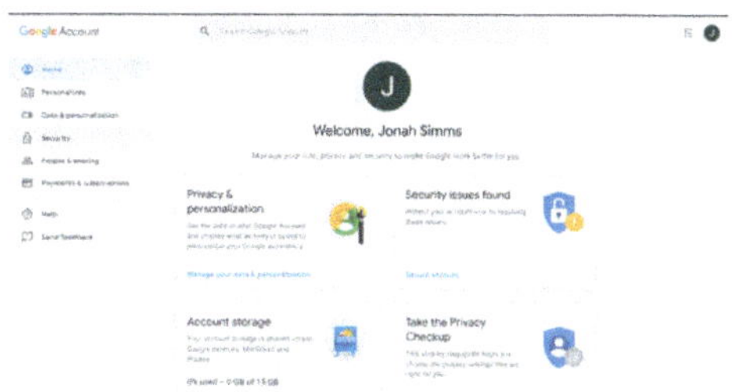

From here, go to Data & personalization:

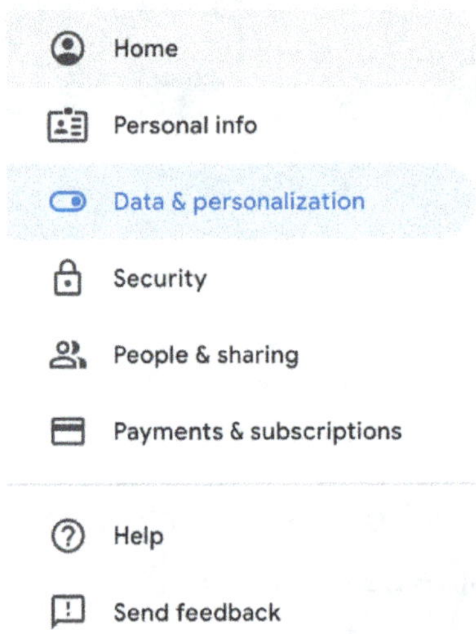

There is a lot here. Scroll down a bit until you get to Download, delete, or make a plan for your data. Next, click Delete a service or your account:

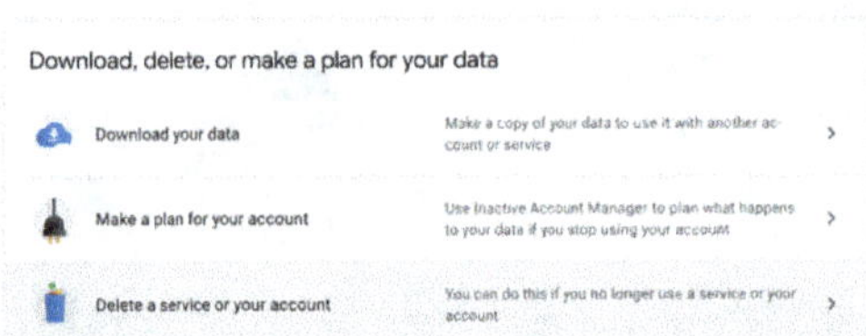

You can delete everything, or you can delete one service in particular—so if you have a YouTube and Gmail account, but only want to delete the Gmail account, then you'd choose service. If you want to go nuclear and delete everything, then delete your Google Account:

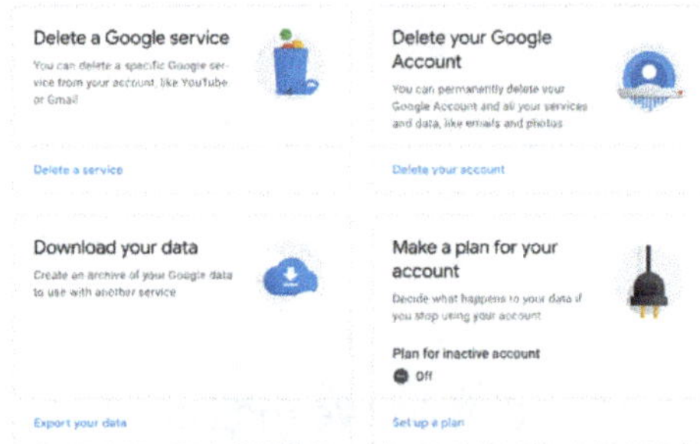

I only have a Gmail account tied to this account, so when I try to delete a service, all I see is Gmail. To delete it, hit the trashcan next to it. Do so at your own risk! This will delete your email and you'll never be able to recover it again!

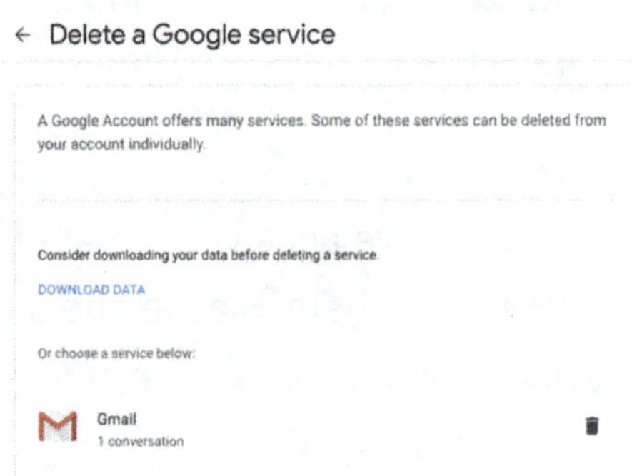

That's it! Gmail in a nutshell! I hope you'll be able to use email in ways you didn't know was possible.

INDEX

About the Author

Scott La Counte is a librarian and writer. His first book, Quiet, Please: Dispatches from a Public Librarian (Da Capo 2008) was the editor's choice for the Chicago Tribune and a Discovery title for the Los Angeles Times; in 2011, he published the YA book The N00b Warriors, which became a #1 Amazon bestseller; his most recent book is #OrganicJesus: Finding Your Way to an Unprocessed, GMO-Free Christianity (Kregel 2016).

He has written dozens of best-selling how-to guides on tech products.

He teaches writing for the Gotham Writers Workshop and UX Design for U.C. Berkeley.

You can connect with him at ScottDouglas.org.

CPSIA information can be obtained
at www.ICGtesting.com
Printed in the USA
LVHW061403281122
733912LV00009B/480

9 781629 175676